Heart of England

Sara Chare

Credits

Footprint credits
Editor: Stephanie Rebello
Production and layout: Emma Bryers
Maps: Kevin Feeney
Cover: Pepi Bluck

Publisher: Patrick Dawson
Managing Editor: Felicity Laughton
Advertising: Elizabeth Taylor
Sales and marketing: Kirsty Holmes

Photography credits
Front cover: Davidmartyn/Dreamstime.com
Back cover: Tupungato/Shutterstock.com

Printed in Great Britain by CPI Antony Rowe,
Chippenham, Wiltshire

MIX
Paper from
responsible sources
FSC® C013604
www.fsc.org

Publishing information
Footprint *Focus Heart of England*
1st edition
© Footprint Handbooks Ltd
April 2013

ISBN: 978 1 909268 17 3
CIP DATA: A catalogue record for this book
is available from the British Library

® Footprint Handbooks and the Footprint
mark are a registered trademark of
Footprint Handbooks Ltd

Published by Footprint
6 Riverside Court
Lower Bristol Road
Bath BA2 3DZ, UK
T +44 (0)1225 469141
F +44 (0)1225 469461
footprinttravelguides.com

Distributed in the USA by Globe Pequot
Press, Guilford, Connecticut

The content of Footprint *Focus Heart
of England* has been updated from
Footprint's *England Handbook*, which
was researched and written by Charlie
Godfrey-Faussett.

Contents

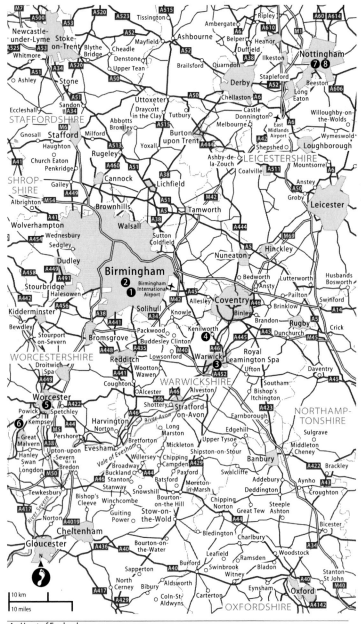

The Heart of England in this book refers to places as diverse as Oxford, Birmingham, Coventry and Church Stretton. Some names may conjure up images of motorways and 1960s' town planning monstrosities, others vibrant student centres and sleepy hamlets. All this is probably true but once you look beyond the obvious there is so much more.

Oxford and Stratford-upon-Avon are firm favourites with overseas and domestic tourists. People come on Shakespeare pilgrimages, to see where Inspector Morse was filmed, to watch a play or to visit the colleges. But did you know that it's not just Oxford that has a Tolkien connection? Those true *Hobbit* and *Lord of the Rings* fans will know that Birmingham can also boast bragging rights. With its excellent shopping, fine Pre-Raphaelite paintings and fascinating Jewellery Quarter, Brum is most firmly on the visitor map these days.

Warwick Castle draws a great many visitors but if you prefer your history more rustic, you may be happier at Kenilworth admiring the ruins. There are also stately homes galore in this part of the country, many managed by National Trust and English Heritage. At Ironside in Shropshire, 'the birthplace of the Industrial Revolution', there are ten museums dedicated to industry, and in Oxford the famous Ashmolean Museum is attracting more visitors than ever since its makeover. If passing through Stoke on Trent a trip to the Wedgewood Visitor Centre should probably be on the cards, and Leicester is capitalizing on the discovery of Richard III's skeleton with a number of exhibitions about the king.

Rustic B&Bs, luxury hotels in listed buildings, Michelin-starred restaurants serving a range of cuisines and excellent curry houses can all be found in the Heart of England. Not forgetting, of course, the cosy locals pubs and the home of the pork pie, Melton Mowbray. If, however, you're just looking to escape from it all, spend a couple of days walking in the Malvern or Shropshire Hills.

Planning your trip

Best time to visit England

The weather in England is generally better between May and September, although it can be gloriously hot in April and cold and damp in August. The west of the country is milder and wetter than the east, and the further north you travel, the colder it becomes.

Transport in England

Compared to the rest of Western Europe, public transport in England is generally poor and can be expensive. Rail, in particular, is expensive and notoriously unreliable. Coach travel is cheaper but much slower, and is further hampered by serious traffic problems around London, Manchester and Birmingham. Some areas are poorly served by public transport of any kind, and if you plan to spend much time in rural areas, it may be worth hiring a car, especially if you are travelling as a couple or group. A useful website for all national public transport information is **Traveline** ① *T0871-200 2233, www.traveline.info*.

Air

England is a small country, and air travel isn't strictly necessary to reach the region. However, with traffic a problem around the cities, some of the cheap fares offered by budget airlines may be attractive. There are good connections between **London** and the regional airports. Bear in mind the time and money it will take you to get to the airport (including check-in times) when deciding whether flying is really going to be a better deal.

Airport information National Express operates a frequent service between London's main airports. **London Heathrow Airport** ① *16 miles west of London between junctions 3 and 4 on the M4, T0844-335 1801, www.heathrowairport.com*, is the world's busiest international airport and it has five terminals, so when leaving London, it's important to check which terminal to go to before setting out for the airport. To get into central London, the cheapest option is the London Underground Piccadilly Line (50 minutes). The fastest option is **Heathrow Express** ① *T0845-6001515, www.heathrowexpress.com*, taking 15-20 minutes. There is a train service **Heathrow Connect** ① *Heathrow T0845-748 4950, www.heathrow connect.com*, which takes 25 minutes. Coaches to destinations all over the country are run by **National Express** ① *T0871-781 8181, www.nationalexpress.com*. There are also buses to Oxford (www.oxfordbus.co.uk), to Reading for trains to Bristol and southwest England (www.railair.com), to Watford for trains to the north of England (www.greenline.co.uk) and to West London (www.tfl.gov.uk). A taxi to central London takes one hour and costs £45-70.

London Gatwick Airport ① *28 miles south of London, off junction 9 on the M23, T0844-892 03222, www.gatwickairport.com*, has two terminals, North and South, with all the usual facilities. To central London, there is the **Gatwick Express** ① *T0845-850 1530, www.gatwickexpress.com, from £17.75 single online*, which takes 30 minutes. **Thameslink** rail services run from King's Cross, Farringdon, Blackfriars and London Bridge stations. Contact **National Rail Enquiries** ① *T0845-748 4950, www.nationalrail.co.uk*, for further information. **EasyBus** (www.easybus.co.uk) is the cheapest option, with prices at £9.99 single, taking just over an hour. A taxi takes a similar time and costs from around £60.

Don't miss...

London City Airport ① *Royal Dock, 6 miles (15 mins' drive) east of the City of London, T020-7646 0000, www.londoncityairport.com*. Take the **Docklands Light Railway** (DLR) to Canning Town (seven minutes) for the **Jubilee line** or a connecting shuttle bus service. A taxi into central London will cost around £35.

London Luton Airport ① *30 miles north of central London, 2 miles off the M1 at junction 10, southeast of Luton, Beds, T01582-405100, www.london-luton.co.uk*. Regular **First Capital Connect** trains run to central London; a free shuttle bus service operates between the airport terminal and the station. **Green Line** ① *www.greenline.co.uk*, coaches run to central London, as does **easyBus** ① *www.easybus.co.uk*. **National Express** ① *www.nationalexpress. com*, operate coaches to many destinations. A taxi takes 50 minutes, costing from £70.

Stansted Airport ① *35 miles northeast of London (near Cambridge) by junction 8 of the M11, T0844-335 1803, www.stanstedairport.com*. **Stansted Express** ① *T0845-600 7245, www.stanstedexpress.com*, runs trains to London's Liverpool Street Station (45 minutes, £22.50 single). **EasyBus** ① *www.easybus.co.uk, from £2*, **Terravision** ① *www.terravision.eu, £9*, and **National Express** ① *www.nationalexpress.com, from £8.50*, run to central London (55 minutes to East London, one hour 30 minutes to Victoria). A taxi to central London takes around an hour to one hour 30 minutes, depending on traffic, and costs around £99.

Manchester International Airport ① *at junction 5 of the M56, T0871-271 0711, www. manchester airport.co.uk*. The airport is well-served by public transport, with trains to and from Manchester Piccadilly as well as direct and connecting services with the Midlands. **National Express** ① *www.nationalexpress.com*, runs routes covering the whole of the UK. A taxi into the city centre should cost around £20.

Birmingham International Airport (BHX) ① *8 miles east of the city centre at junction 6 on the M42, T0871-222 0072, www.birminghamairport.co.uk*. A taxi into the centre should cost from £25. Several trains per hour run the free 10-minute Air-Rail Link to Birmingham International Station, and other connections across England and Wales can be made by rail or coach, with **National Express** ① *www.nationalexpress.com*.

Rail

National Rail Enquiries ① *T08457-484950, www.nationalrail.co.uk*, are quick and courteous with information on rail services and fares but not always accurate, so double check. They can't book tickets but will provide you with the relevant telephone number. The website, www.thetrainline.co.uk, also shows prices clearly.

Railcards There are a variety of railcards which give discounts on fares for certain groups. Cards are valid for one year and most are available from main stations. You need two passport photos and proof of age or status. A Young Person's Railcard is for those aged 16-25 or full-time students aged 26+ in the UK. Costs £28 for one year and gives 33% discount on most train tickets and some other services (www.16-25railcard.co.uk). A Senior Citizen's Railcard is for those aged over 60, is the same price and offers the same discounts as a Young Person's Railcard (www.senior-railcard.co.uk). A Disabled Person's Railcard costs £20 and gives 33% discount to a disabled person and one other. Pick up an application form from stations and send it to Disabled Person's Railcard Office, PO Box 11631, Laurencekirk AB30 9AA. It may take up to 10 working days to be delivered, so apply in advance (www.disabledpersons-railcard.co.uk). A Family & Friends Railcard costs £28 and gives 33% discount on most tickets for up to four adults travelling together, and 60% discount for up to four children. It's available to buy online as well as in most stations.

Road

Bus and coach Travelling by bus takes longer than the train but is much cheaper. Road links between cities and major towns in England are excellent, traffic jams notwithstanding, but far less frequent in more remote rural areas. A number of companies offer express coach services day and night. The main operator is **National Express** ① *T08717-818178, www. nationalexpress.com*, which has a nationwide network with over 1000 destinations. Tickets can be bought at bus stations, from a huge number of agents throughout the country or online. Sample return fares if booked in advance: London to Nottingham (two hours, 20 minutes) £40, London to Birmingham (one hour, 30 minutes) £15. **Megabus** ① *T0900-1600 900 (61p per min from BT landlines, calls from other networks may be higher), www. megabus.com*, is a cheaper alternative with a more limited service.

Full-time students, those aged under 25 or over 60 or those registered disabled, can buy a **coach card** for £10 which is valid for one year and gets you a 30% discount on all fares. Children normally travel for half price, but with a Family Card costing £16, two children travel free with two adults. Available to overseas passport holders, the **Brit Xplorer Pass** offers unlimited travel on all National Express buses. Passes cost from £79 for seven days, £139 for 14 days and £219 for its month-long Rolling Stone pass. They can be bought from major airports and bus terminals.

Car Travelling with your own private transport allows you to cover a lot of ground in a short space of time and to reach rural places. The main disadvantages are rising fuel costs, parking and traffic congestion. The latter is particularly heavy on the M25 which encircles London, the M6 around Birmingham. The M4 and M5 motorways to the West Country can also become choked at weekends and bank holidays.

Motoring organizations can help with route planning, traffic advice, insurance and breakdown cover. The two main ones are: the **Automobile Association (AA)** ① *T0800-085 2721, emergency number T0800-887766, www.theaa.com*, which offers a year's breakdown cover starting at £38, and the **Royal Automobile Club (RAC)** ① *T0844-273 4341, emergency number T08000-828282, www.rac.co.uk*, which has a year's breakdown cover starting at £31.99. Both have cover for emergency assistance. You can still call the emergency numbers if you're not a member, but you'll have to a pay a large fee.

Car hire Car hire is expensive and the minimum you can expect to pay is around £100 per week for a small car. Always check and compare conditions, such as mileage limitations, excess payable in the case of an accident, etc. Small, local hire companies often offer better deals than the larger multinationals. Most companies prefer payment with a credit card – some insist on it – otherwise you'll have to leave a large deposit (£100 or more). You need to have had a full driver's licence for at least a year and to be aged between 21 (25 for some companies) and 70.

Bicycle   Cycling is a pleasant if slightly hazardous way to see the area. Although conditions for cyclists are improving, with a growing network of cycle lanes in cities, most other roads do not have designated cycle paths, and cyclists are not allowed on motorways. You can load your bike onto trains, though some restrictions apply during rush hour. See www.ctc. org.uk for information on routes, restrictions and facilities.

Where to stay in England

Accommodation can mean anything from being pampered to within an inch of your life in a country house spa hotel to glamping in a yurt. If you have the money, then the sky is very much the limit in terms of sheer splendour and excess. We have listed top class establishments in this book, with a bias towards those that offer that little bit extra in terms of character.

But we have tried to give as broad a selection as possible to cater for all tastes and budgets but if you can't find what you're after, or if someone else has beaten you to the draw, then the tourist information centres (TICs) will help find accommodation for you. Some offices charge a small fee (usually £1) for booking a room, while others ask you to pay a deposit of 10% which is deducted from your first night's bill. Details of town and city TICs are given throughout the guide.

Accommodation will be your greatest expense, particularly if you are travelling on your own. Single rooms are in short supply and many places are reluctant to let a double room to one person, even when they're not busy. Single rooms are usually more than the cost per person for a double room and sometimes cost the same as two people sharing a double room.

Hotels, guesthouses and B&Bs

Area tourist boards publish accommodation lists that include campsites, hostels, self-catering accommodation, hotels, guesthouses and bed and breakfasts (B&Bs). Places participating in the VisitEngland system will have a plaque displayed outside which shows their grading, determined by a number of stars ranging from one to five. These reflect the level of facilities, as well as the quality of hospitality and service. However, do not assume that a B&B, guesthouse or hotel is no good because it is not listed by the tourist board. They simply don't want to pay to be included in the system, and some of them may offer better value.

Hotels   At the top end of the scale there are some fabulously luxurious hotels, some in beautiful locations. Some are converted mansions or castles, and offer a chance to enjoy a taste of aristocratic grandeur and style. At the lower end of the scale, there is often little to choose between cheaper hotels and guesthouses or B&Bs. The latter often offer higher standards of comfort and a more personal service, but many smaller hotels are really just guesthouses, and are often family run and every bit as friendly. Rooms in most mid-range to expensive hotels almost always have bathrooms en suite. Many upmarket hotels offer

Price codes

Where to stay

££££ over £160   **£££** £90-160

££ £50-90   **£** under £50

Prices include taxes and service charge, but not meals. They are based on a double room in high season.

Restaurants

£££ over £30   **££** £15-30   **£** under £15

Prices refer to the cost of a two-course meal, without a drink.

excellent room-only deals in the low season. An efficient last-minute hotel booking service is www.laterooms.com, which specializes in weekend breaks. Also note that many hotels offer cheaper rates for online booking through agencies such as www.lastminute.com.

Guesthouses Guesthouses are often large, converted family homes with up to five or six rooms. They tend to be slightly more expensive than B&Bs, charging between £30 and £50 per person per night, and though they are often less personal, usually provide better facilities, such as en suite bathroom, TV in each room, free Wi-Fi and private parking. Many guesthouses offer evening meals, though this may have to be requested in advance.

Bed and breakfasts (B&Bs) B&Bs usually provide the cheapest private accommodation. At the bottom end of the scale you can get a bedroom in a private house, a shared bathroom and a huge cooked breakfast from around £25 per person per night. Small B&Bs may only have one or two rooms to let, so it's important to book in advance during the summer season. More upmarket B&Bs, some in handsome period houses, have en suite bathrooms, free Wi-Fi and TVs in each room and usually charge from £35 per person per night.

Hostels

For those travelling on a tight budget, there is a network of hostels offering cheap accommodation in major cities, national parks and other areas of beauty run by the **Youth Hostel Association (YHA)** ① *T01629-592600, or customer services T0800-0191 700, +44-1629 592700 from outside the UK, www.yha.org.uk*. Membership costs from £14.35 a year and a bed in a dormitory costs £15-25 a night. They offer bunk-bed accommodation in single-sex dormitories or smaller rooms, as well as family rooms, kitchen and laundry facilities. Though some rural hostels are still strict on discipline and impose a 2300 curfew, those in larger towns and cities tend to be more relaxed and doors are closed as late as 0200. Some larger hostels provide breakfasts for around £2.50 and three-course evening meals for £4-5. You should always phone ahead, as many hostels are closed during the day and phone numbers are listed in this guide. Advance booking is recommended at all times, particularly from May to September and on public holidays. Many hostels are closed during the winter. Youth hostel members are entitled to various discounts, including tourist attractions and travel. The YHA also offer budget self-catering bunkhouses with mostly dorm accommodation and some family rooms, which are in more rural locations. Camping barns, camping pods and camping are other options offered by the YHA; see the website for details.

Details of most independent hostels can be found in the *Independent Hostel Guide* (T01629-580427, www.independenthostelguide.co.uk). Independent hostels tend to be more laid-back, with fewer rules and no curfew, and no membership is required. They all have dorms, hot showers and self-catering kitchens, and some have family and double rooms. Some include continental breakfast, or offer cheap breakfasts.

Self-catering accommodation

There are lots of different types of accommodation to choose from, to suit all budgets, ranging from luxury lodges, castles and lighthouses to basic cottages. Expect to pay at least £200-400 per week for a two-bedroom cottage in the winter, rising to £400-1000 in the high season, or more if it's a particularly nice place. A good source of information on self-catering accommodation is the VisitEngland website, www.visitengland.com, and its *VisitEngland Self-catering 2013* guide, which lists many properties and is available to buy from any tourist office and many bookshops, but there are also dozens of excellent websites to browse. Amongst the best websites are: www.cottages4you.co.uk, www. ruralretreats.co.uk and www.ownersdirect.co.uk. If you want to tickle a trout or feed a pet lamb, **Farm Stay UK** ① *www.farmstay.co.uk*, offer over a thousand good value rural places to stay around England, all clearly listed on a clickable map.

More interesting places to stay are offered by the **Landmark Trust** ① *T01628-825925, www.landmarktrust.org.uk*, who rent out renovated historic landmark buildings, from atmospheric castles to cottages, and the **National Trust** ① *T0844-800 2070, www. nationaltrustcottages.co.uk*, who provide a wide variety of different accommodation on their estates. A reputable agent for self-catering cottages is **English Country Cottages** ① *T0845-268 0785, www.english-country-cottages.co.uk*.

Campsites

Campsites vary greatly in quality and level of facilities. Some sites are only open from April to October. See the following sites: www.pitchup.com; www.coolcamping.com, good for finding characterful sites that allow campfires; www.ukcampsite.co.uk, which is the most comprehensive service with thousands of sites, many with pictures and reviews from punters; and www.campingandcaravanningclub.co.uk. The Forestry Commission have campsites on their wooded estates, see www.campingintheforest.com.

Food and drink in England

Food

Only 30 years ago few would have thought to come to England for haute cuisine. Since the 1980s, though, the English have been determinedly shrugging off their reputation for over-boiled cabbage and watery beef. Now cookery shows such as *Masterchef* are the most popular on TV, after the soaps, and thanks in part to the wave of celebrity chefs they have created, you can expect a generally high standard of competence in restaurant kitchens. Ludlow has carved itself a reputation almost solely on the strength of its cuisine.

Pub food has also been transformed in recent years, and now many of them offer ambitious lunchtime and supper menus in so-called gastro pubs. The biggest problem with eating out is the ludicrously limited serving hours in some pubs and hotels, particularly in remoter locations. These places only serve food during restricted hours, generally about 1200-1430 for lunch and 1830-2130 for supper, seemingly ignorant of the eating habits of foreign visitors, or those who would prefer a bit more flexibility during their holiday. In small places especially, it can be difficult finding food outside these enforced times. Places that serve food all day till 2100 or later are restaurants, fast-food outlets and the many chic bistros and café-bars, which can be found not only in the main cities but increasingly in smaller towns. The latter often offer very good value and above-average quality fare.

Drink

Drinking is a national hobby and sometimes a dangerous one at that. **Real ale** – flat, brown **beer** known as **bitter**, made with hops – is the national drink and, although undergoing something of a resurgence, still struggles to maintain its market share in the face of fierce competition from continental lagers and alcopops. Many small independent breweries are still up and running, as well as microbreweries attached to individual **pubs**, which produce far superior ales. **Cider** (fermented apple juice) is also experiencing a resurgence of interest and is a speciality of Somerset. English **wine** is also proving surprisingly resilient: generally it compares favourably with German varieties and many vineyards now offer continental-style sampling sessions.

In many pubs the basic ales are chilled under gas pressure like lagers, but the best ales, such as those from the independents, are 'real ales', still fermenting in the cask and served cool but not chilled (around 12°C) under natural pressure from a handpump, electric pump or air pressure fount.

The **pub** is still the traditional place to enjoy a drink: the best are usually freehouses (not tied to a brewery) and feature real log or coal fires in winter, flower-filled gardens for the summer (even in cities occasionally) and, most importantly, thriving local custom. Many also offer characterful accommodation and restaurants serving high-quality fare. Pubs are prey to the same market forces as any other business, though, and many a delightful local has recently succumbed to exorbitant property prices or to the bland makeover favoured by the large chains. In 2012, pubs were closing at the rate of 12 a week due to the recession.

Essentials A-Z

Accident and emergency
For police, fire brigade, ambulance and, in certain areas, mountain rescue or coastguard, T999 or T112.

Disabled travellers
Wheelchair users, and blind or partially sighted people are automatically given 34-50% discount on train fares, and those with other disabilities are eligible for the **Disabled Person's Railcard**, which costs £20 per year and gives a third off most tickets. If you will need assistance at a railway station, call the train company that manages the station you're starting your journey from 24 hrs in advance. Disabled UK residents can apply to their local councils for a concessionary bus pass. **National Express** have a helpline for disabled passengers, T08717-818179, to plan journeys and arrange assistance. They also sell a discount coach card for £10 for people with disabilities.

The **English Tourist Board** website, www.visitengland.com, has information on the National Accessible Scheme (NAS) logos to help disabled travellers find the right accommodation for their needs, as well as details of walks that are possible with wheelchairs and the Shopmobility scheme. Many local tourist offices offer accessibility details for their area.

Useful organizations include:
Radar, T020-7250 3222, www.radar.org.uk. A good source of advice and information. It produces an annual National Key Scheme Guide and key for gaining access to over 9000 toilet facilities across the UK.
Tourism for all, T0845-124 9971, www.holidaycare.org.uk, www.tourismforall.org.uk. An excellent source of information about travel and for identifying accessible accommodation in the UK.

Electricity
The current in Britain is 240V AC. Plugs have 3 square pins and adapters are widely available.

Health
For minor accidents go to the nearest casualty department or an Accident and Emergency (A&E) Unit at a hospital. For other enquiries phone NHS Direct 24 hrs (T0845-4647) or visit an NHS walk-in centre. See also individual town and city directories throughout the book for details of local medical services.

Money → *For up-to-date exhange rates, see www.xe.com.*
The British currency is the pound sterling (£), divided into 100 pence (p). Coins come in denominations of 1p, 2p, 5p, 10p, 20p, 50p, £1 and £2. Banknotes come in denominations of £5, £10, £20 and £50. The last of these notes are not widely used and may be difficult to change.

Banks and bureaux de change
Banks tend to offer similar exchange rates and are usually the best places to change money and cheques. Outside banking hours you'll have to use a bureau de change, which can be easily found at the airports and train stations and in larger cities. **Thomas Cook** and other major travel agents also operate bureaux de change with reasonable rates. Avoid changing money or cheques in hotels, as the rates are usually poor. Main post offices and branches of **Marks and Spencer** will change cash without charging commission.

Cost of travelling
England can be an expensive place to visit. There is budget accommodation available, however, and backpackers will be able to keep their costs down. Fuel is a major expense

and won't just cost an arm and a leg but also the limbs of all remaining family members, and public transport – particularly rail travel if not booked in advance – can also be pricey, especially for families. Accommodation and restaurant prices also tend to be higher in more popular destinations and during the busy summer months.

The minimum daily budget required, if you're staying in hostels or camping, cycling or hitching (not recommended), and cooking your own meals, will be around £30 per person per day. If you start using public transport and eating out occasionally that will rise to around £35-40. Those staying in slightly more upmarket B&Bs or guesthouses, eating out every evening at pubs or modest restaurants and visiting tourist attractions can expect to pay around £60 per day. If you also want to hire a car and eat well, then costs will rise considerably to at least £75-80 per person per day. Single travellers will have to pay more than half the cost of a double room, and should budget on spending around 60-70% of what a couple would spend.

Credit cards and ATMs
Most hotels, shops and restaurants accept the major credit cards though some places may charge for using them. Some smaller establishments such as B&Bs may only accept cash.

Currency cards
If you don't want to carry lots of cash, prepaid currency cards allow you to preload money from your bank account, fixed at the day's exchange rate. They look like a credit or debit card and are issued by specialist money changing companies, such as Travelex and Caxton FX. You can top up and check your balance by phone, online and sometimes by text.

Money transfers
If you need money urgently, the quickest way to have it sent to you is to have it wired to the nearest bank via **Western Union**, T0800-833 833, www.westernunion.co.uk, or **MoneyGram**, www.moneygram.com. The Post Office can also arrange a MoneyGram transfer. Charges are on a sliding scale; so it will cost proportionately less to wire out more money. Money can also be wired by **Thomas Cook**, www.thomasexchangeglobal.co.uk, or transferred via a bank draft, but this can take up to a week.

Taxes
Most goods are subject to a Value Added Tax (VAT) of 20%, with the major exception of food and books. VAT is usually already included in the advertised price of goods. Visitors from non-EU countries can save money through shopping at places that offer Tax Free Shopping (also known as the Retail Export Scheme), which allows a refund of VAT on goods that will be taken out of the country. Note that not all shops participate in the scheme and that VAT cannot be reclaimed on hotel bills or other services.

Opening hours
Businesses are usually open Mon-Sat 0900-1700. In towns and cities, as well as villages in holiday areas, many shops open on a Sun but they will open later and close earlier. For banks, see above. For TIC opening hours, see the tourist information sections in the relevant cities, towns and villages in the text.

Post
Most post offices are open Mon-Fri 0900 to 1730 and Sat 0900-1230 or 1300. Smaller sub-post offices are closed for an hour at lunch (1300-1400) and many of them operate out of a shop. Stamps can be bought at post offices, but also from many shops. A 1st-class letter weighing up to 100 g to anywhere in the UK costs 60p (a large letter over 240 mm by 165 mm is 90p) and should arrive the following day, while 2nd-class letters weighing up to 100 g cost 50p (69p) and take between 2-4 days. For more information about Royal

Mail postal services, call T08457-740740, or visit www.royalmail.com.

Safety
Generally speaking, England is a safe place to visit. English cities have their fair share of crime, but much of it is drug-related and confined to the more deprived peripheral areas. Trust your instincts, and if in doubt, take a taxi.

Telephone → *Country code +44.*
Useful numbers: operator T100; international operator T155; directory enquiries T192; overseas directory enquiries T153.

Most public payphones are operated by **British Telecom** (**BT**) and can be found in towns and cities, though less so in rural areas. Numbers of public phone booths have declined in recent years due to the advent of the mobile phone, so don't rely on being able to find a payphone wherever you go. Calls from BT payphones cost a minimum of 60p, for which you get 30 mins for a local or national call. Calls to non-geographic numbers (eg 0845), mobile phones and others may cost more. Payphones (few and far between these days) take either coins (10p, 20p, 50p and £1), 50c, 1 or 2 euro coins, credit cards or BT Chargecards, which are available at newsagents and post offices displaying the BT logo. These cards come in denominations of £2, £3, £5 and £10. Some payphones also have facilities for internet, text messaging and emailing.

For most countries (including Europe, USA and Canada) calls are cheapest Mon-Fri between 1800 and 0800 and all day Sat-Sun. For Australia and New Zealand it's cheapest to call from 1430-1930 and from 2400-0700 every day. However, the cheapest ways to call abroad from England is not via a standard UK landline provider. Calls are free using **Skype** on the internet, or you can route calls from your phone through the internet with **JaJah** (www.jajah.com) or from a mobile using **Rebtel**. Many phone companies offer discounted call rates by calling their access number prior to dialling the number you want, including www.dialabroad.co.uk and www.simply-call.com.

Area codes are not needed if calling from within the same area. Any number prefixed by 0800 or 0500 is free to the caller; 08457 numbers are charged at local rates and 08705 numbers at the national rate.

Time
Greenwich Mean Time (GMT) is used from late Oct to late Mar, after which time the clocks go forward 1 hr to British Summer Time (BST).

Tipping
Tipping in England is at the customer's discretion. In a restaurant it is customary to leave a tip of 10-15% if you are satisfied with the service. If the bill already includes a service charge, which is likely if you are in a large group, you needn't add a further tip. Tipping is not normal in pubs or bars. Taxi drivers may expect a tip for longer journeys, usually around 10%.

Tourist information
Tourist information centres (TICs) can be found in most towns. Their addresses, phone numbers and opening hours are listed in the relevant sections of this book. Opening hours vary depending on the time of year, and many of the smaller offices are closed or have limited opening hours during the winter months. All tourist offices provide information on accommodation, public transport, local attractions and restaurants, as well as selling books, local guides, maps and souvenirs. Many also have free street plans and leaflets describing local walks. They can also book accommodation for a small fee.

Museums, galleries and historic houses
Over 300 stately homes, gardens and countryside areas are cared for by the **National Trust** ① *T0844-800 1895, www.nationaltrust.org.uk.* If you're going

to be visiting several sights during your stay, then it's worth taking annual membership, which costs £53, £25 if you're aged under 26 and £70 for a family, giving free access to all National Trust properties. A similar organization is **English Heritage** ① *T0870-333 1181, www.english-heritage.org.uk*, which manages hundreds of ancient monuments and other sights around England, including Stonehenge, and focuses on restoration and preservation. Membership includes free admission to sites, and advance information on events, and costs £47 per adult to £82 per couple, under-19s free. **Natural England** ① *T0845-600 3078, www.naturalengland.org.uk*, is concerned with restoring and conserving the English countryside, and can give information on walks and events in the countryside.

Many other historic buildings are owned by local authorities, and admission is cheap, or in many cases free. Most municipal **art galleries** and **museums** are free, as well as most state-owned museums, particularly those in London and other large cities. Most fee-paying attractions give a discount or concession for senior citizens, the unemployed, full-time students and children under 16 (those under 5 are admitted free in most places). Proof of age or status must be shown.

Finding out more

The best way of finding out more information is to contact Visit England (aka the English Tourist Board), www.visitengland.com. Alternatively, you can contact VisitBritain, the organization responsible for tourism. Both organizations can provide a wealth of free literature and information such as maps, city guides and accommodation brochures. Travellers with special needs should also contact VisitEngland or their nearest VisitBritain office. If you want more detailed information on a particular area, contact the specific tourist boards; see in the main text for details.

Visas and immigration

Visa regulations are subject to change, so it is essential to check with your local British embassy, high commission or consulate before leaving home. Citizens of all European countries – except Albania, Bosnia Herzegovina, Kosovo, Macedonia, Moldova, Turkey, Serbia and all former Soviet republics (other than the Baltic states) – require only a passport to enter Britain and can generally stay for up to 3 months. Citizens of Australia, Canada, New Zealand, South Africa or the USA can stay for up to 6 months, providing they have a return ticket and sufficient funds to cover their stay. Citizens of most other countries require a visa from the commission or consular office in the country of application.

The **UK Border Agency**, www.ukba.homeoffice.gov.uk, is responsible for UK immigration matters and its website is a good place to start for anyone hoping visit, work, study or emigrate to the UK. For visa extensions also contact the UK Border Agency via the website. Citizens of Australia, Canada, New Zealand, South Africa or the USA wishing to stay longer than 6 months will need an Entry Clearance Certificate from the British High Commission in their country. For more details, contact your nearest British embassy, consulate or high commission, or the Foreign and Commonwealth Office in London.

Weights and measures

Imperial and metric systems are both in use. Distances on roads are measured in miles and yards, drinks poured in pints and gills, but generally, the metric system is used elsewhere.

Contents

Footprint features

Heart of England

Birmingham

Perhaps because for too many years Birmingham has been the butt of many a comedian's joke about smoking chimneys and heavy metal music, people are surprised to learn that it is Britain's second city. It's easy to be snobbish about Birmingham – it's easy to be a Birmophobe or sniffy about where it gets the money to maintain such splendid facilities as Birmingham City Museum and Art Gallery and the Barber Institute, and many people are. But ironically, heavy metal in the form of iron, steel and particularly gold and silver has played a very important part in the town's development and still does. Birmingham, or Brummagem as it is colloquially known, has a world-famous jewellery quarter and as for the smoking chimneys, it's worth remembering that Birmingham has more trees than people, over a million. It's also probably Britain's most racially integrated city, with Chinese, Sikh, Muslim, Hindu, Irish, Jewish and Afro-Caribbean communities. With a number of Michelin-starred restaurants, Birmingham is firmly on the food-lovers' trail; in 2012 the *New York Times* named it among the top 20 destinations to visit due to its culinary reputation. Over 33 million visitors came to Birmingham in 2011 and since the 1970s, when the mighty Spaghetti Junction made Brum synonymous with pollution, the city has really cleaned up its act, in more ways than one.

Arriving in Birmingham

Getting there

Birmingham Airport ⓘ *www.birminghamairport.co.uk*, is one of the busiest airports in the UK with many of the low-cost airlines including it on their itinerary. It's handy for the NEC and Birmingham International Train Station where there are regular trains to the centre of town and New Street Station. **Birmingham New Street** station has a strong claim to be the most central **train** station in the country. **Virgin Trains** operate three services daily from London Euston (just under 1½ hours) every day. There's also a slower, more picturesque and cheaper **London Midland** ⓘ *www.londonmidland.com*, service (2¼ hours) running from Euston twice every hour throughout the week and at weekends. If you want to go to Birmingham by an even more rural and more leisurely route catch a train from the spectacular Marylebone Station, London, operated by **Chiltern Railways** ⓘ *www.chilternrailways.co.uk*, to Birmingham Moor Street. This is also an excellent way to explore the surrounding countryside including Warwick and Royal Leamington Spa.

Being famous as the meeting point of three **motorways**, you can get to Birmingham by car easily. From the south take either the M40 from London via Oxford or the M5 from Bristol. From the north take the M6. From the West take the M54 past Wolverhampton where it joins the M6 at Junction 10a. There is also the M6 Toll (see www.m6toll.co.uk for current prices), which runs for 27 miles from junction 3a of the M6 to junction 11a. You can also join it from the M42. Birmingham city centre is well served with around 20 long-stay multi-storey car parks. Street parking is relatively easy and after 1800 free in many spots, there are also special evening rates at some car parks.

Getting around

Buses are one of the best ways to see and get around Birmingham, with day savers available for £3.90 which allow unlimited travel on all **National Express West Midlands** buses or £8 for 5 people and unlimited travel. The 50 bus is particularly good: it starts on Moor Street near Selfridges and will take you through a cool nightclub area (Digbeth), then through Moseley with its fantastic hippy pubs and Tolkien connections and eventually to the Maypole, which is in spitting distance of the Lickey Hills. For more details or to plan your journey, see www.nxbus.co.uk.

There is a **London Midland** ⓘ *www.londonmidland.com*, **train** service from New Street, which is good for trips to the Black Country and the wonderful Walsall Art Gallery. Services also run to Leamington, as well as a number of local destinations.

The Metro ⓘ *www.nxbus.co.uk/the-metro*, is a light rail system that runs between Snow Street Station in Birmingham and Wolverhampton.

A useful reference for planning how to get around Birmingham and the surrounding area by bus, train and Metro is the Network West Midlands website. They sell combination tickets, such as Travel Without Limits (rail, Metro and bus travel).

Information

The **visitor centres** ⓘ *Junction of New St and Corporation St, B2 4DB, Mon-Sat 0900-1700, Sun 1000-1600; Birmingham Airport Arrivals, Mon-Sun 0700-2000*, are all managed by **Marketing Birmingham** ⓘ *www.visitbirmingham.com*. They can be contacted on T0844-888 3883 and offer a free accommodation booking service, as well as the usual maps and guides.

Birmingham

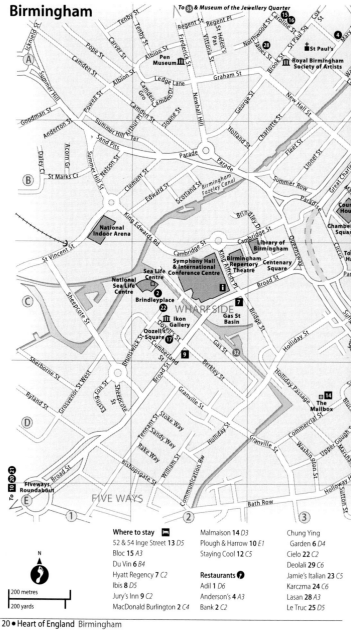

To ⑩ & Museum of the Jewellery Quarter

To ⑩

Where to stay 🛏

52 & 54 Inge Street **13** *D5*
Bloc **15** *A3*
Du Vin **6** *B4*
Hyatt Regency **7** *C2*
Ibis **8** *D5*
Jury's Inn **9** *C2*
MacDonald Burlington **2** *C4*

Malmaison **14** *D3*
Plough & Harrow **10** *E1*
Staying Cool **12** *C5*

Restaurants 🍴

Adil **1** *D6*
Anderson's **4** *A3*
Bank **2** *C2*

Chung Ying
  Garden **6** *D4*
Cielo **22** *C2*
Deolali **29** *C6*
Jamie's Italian **23** *C5*
Karczma **24** *C6*
Lasan **28** *A3*
Le Truc **25** *D5*

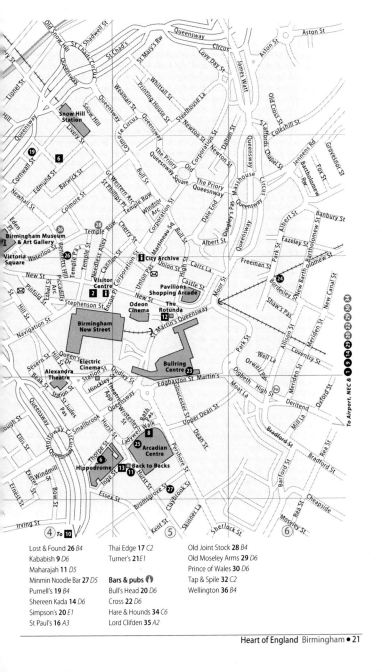

Lost & Found **26** *B4*
Kababish **9** *D6*
Maharajah **11** *D5*
Minmin Noodle Bar **27** *D5*
Purnell's **19** *B4*
Shereen Kada **14** *D6*
Simpson's **20** *E1*
St Paul's **16** *A3*

Thai Edge **17** *C2*
Turner's **21** *E1*

Bars & pubs 🍷
Bull's Head **20** *D6*
Cross **22** *D6*
Hare & Hounds **34** *C6*
Lord Clifden **35** *A2*

Old Joint Stock **28** *B4*
Old Moseley Arms **29** *D6*
Prince of Wales **30** *D6*
Tap & Spile **32** *C2*
Wellington **36** *B4*

History

Birmingham is laced with canals – 32 miles compared to Venice's 28 miles – and the city is justifiably proud of its claim to be the cradle of the Industrial Revolution. The world's first steam engines were built in Birmingham by Boulton and Watt and the city is littered with fascinating sites of industrial heritage, most of them accessible by leisurely canal trips, which start in Brindleyplace, easily accessible from New Street Station. Known as the 'workshop of the world', Birmingham nurtured cutting-edge manufacturing from jewellery to chocolate for over three centuries. More recently Birmingham became Britain's Motown, with the Leyland Longbridge plant originating the Mini, the ultimate icon of Britcool. That was before the second industrial revolution, when Mrs Thatcher smashed the unions and Birmingham became known for the ferocity of its strikes and a symbol of all that was wrong with British industry. This was a period where Brum flourished more as a cultural centre spawning bands such as Slade, The Electric Light Orchestra and the immortal Black Sabbath, fronted by the unforgettable Ozzy Osbourne, probably now the most famous Brummie in the world – certainly the only Brummie to have bitten the head off a bat *and* been personally invited to the White House by a US President (although Birmingham did play host to Clinton during a G8 summit). Now Birmingham has evolved – some would say beyond all recognition – from its old industrial past into a new industries future where huge conferences and tourism lie at the heart of the city's success.

Places in Birmingham → *For listings, see pages 26-31.*

Victoria Square and the Museum and Art Gallery

For a fresh-out-of New Street introduction to the city and all it has to offer walk up pedestrianized New Street to Victoria Square, where there is one of the largest fountains in Europe featuring a rampant naked lady and about 3000 gallons of water. Nicknamed **'The Floozie in the Jacuzzi'**, all Brummies know where this is and the square affords great views of **The Council House** ① *guided tours can be arranged, Democratic.Services@birmingham.gov. uk or T0121-303 2438*, a fine building which features a proud mural of Britannia rewarding the manufacturers of Birmingham. This is also where you'll find Anthony Gormley's statue *Iron: Man*, or The Iron Man as it's called locally. On the other side of the square stands **The Town Hall**, a magnificent replica of the Temple of Castor and Pollux in Rome. As the former home of the City of Birmingham Symphony Orchestra, it's a building rich in musical heritage having played host to musos as diverse as Elgar and The Beatles. It reopened in 2007 after extensive renovations and once again hosts musical performances.

Round the corner from The Council House is **Birmingham Museum and Art Gallery** ① *Chamberlain Sq, B3 3DH, T0121-303 1966, www.bmag.org.uk, Mon-Thu 1000-1700, Fri 1030-1700, Sat 1000-1700, Sun 1230-1700, free, some exhibitions may charge.* With one of the world's finest collections of Pre-Raphaelite art, the roomy galleries allow you to relive DG Rossetti's obsession with the opium-addled Miss Siddall, the foremost Pre-Raphaelite model. Other Pre-Raphaelite highlights include Edward Burne-Jones' mighty *Star of Bethlehem*, one of the largest paintings you will see anywhere and his tapestry collaborations with Arts and Crafts head honcho William Morris. The museum is also home to the fascinating **Staffordshire Hoard** ① *www.staffordshirehoard.org.uk*, Anglo-Saxon gold treasures found in 2009 in Hammerwich, near Lichfield.

True to the city's manufacturing heritage, there's also a terrific **Applied Arts Collection** featuring a treasure trove of enough ornamental gold and silver to fuel a dozen heist movies. Other unexpected delights include Jacob Epstein's brilliant sculpture *Lucifer* presiding magisterially over the Museum Shop and the Edwardian Tearoom. The **Waterhall Gallery** contains the modern art collection.

Centenary Square and Broad Street

Passing through Chamberlain Square with the Central Library on the right (a monstrosity likened by some to a bus shelter) and crossing the inappropriately named Paradise Circus you come to **Centenary Square** with the **International Conference Centre** ① *T0121-644 5025, www.theicc.co.uk*, and **Symphony Hall** (see page 29) adjoining the top end of **Broad Street**. This is also where the new **Library of Birmingham** will open in September 2013, the old building being demolished to make way for redevelopment.

While the City of Birmingham Symphony Orchestra (CBSO), transformed by Simon Rattle into one of the top 10 orchestras in the world and housed in Symphony Hall, offers supremely civilized entertainment, Broad Street marks the beginning of around a mile of bars, clubs and night spots.

Brindleyplace

Passing swiftly through the ICC atrium, you emerge into an area known as **Wharfside** which is the entrance to one of the city's smartest canalside developments, **Brindleyplace** ① *www.brindleyplace.com*. Though primarily a destination for Brum's glitterati, there's also the Norman Foster-designed **National SEA LIFE Centre** ① *The Waters Edge, Brindleyplace, B1 2HL, T0871-423 2110, www.visitsealife.com, Mon-Fri 1000-1700, Sat-Sun 1000-18*. This is the kind of place kids love, especially the 360° tank where sharks appear to surround you.

For more grown-up tastes, across the square from SEA LIFE is **The Ikon Gallery** ① *1 Oozell's Sq, B1 2HS, T0121-248 0708, Tue-Sun 1100-1800, free*, which has long enjoyed – some say without justification – the reputation as a leading European contemporary art gallery. What isn't disputed is that it's one of the best restorations of a 19th-century school building in the country, with a wonderful exhibition space.

Gas Street Basin and the Canals

Brindleyplace has sensitively restored an area that had been synonymous with industrial grime for hundreds of years – it was the 19th-century equivalent of the spaghetti junction, whereby coal from the mines in the Black Country was transported to and through Birmingham. The hub of Brum's canal world is the superbly preserved Gas Street Basin, a few minutes' walk from Brindleyplace by the side of the canal where you can relax by the water. From here you can also see the imposing **Cube building**, which houses flats, shops, restaurants and a hotel.

The Canal Shop provides canal tours through **Second City Canal Cruises Limited** ① *T0121-236 9811, M07891 061289; tours from 1 hr to day trips*. Phone before coming down to check trips are running. For posher boats with bars on them you could try **Sherborne Wharf Heritage Narrowboats** ① *Sherborne St, B16 8DE, T0121-455 6163*.

The Jewellery Quarter
① *www.jewelleryquarter.net*.
If you're not yet sick of canals, a fun way to get to this extraordinary and historic industrial centre and the largest working jewellery quarter in Europe is on the canal towpath from Brindleyplace. Turn right at the National Indoor Arena onto the Birmingham Fazeley Canal, passing eight locks for access into New Hall Street, which will take you to **St Paul**

Square, Hockley. This is Birmingham's last remaining entirely Georgian square. As well as containing the exquisite **St Paul's Church** ① *www.saintpaulbrum.org*, the square has become an increasingly affluent destination for bar and restaurant-goers.

A perfect way to digest your lunch is to visit the **Royal Birmingham Society of Artists** ① *4 Brook St, St Paul's Sq, B3 1SA, T0121-236 4353, www.rbsa.org.uk, Mon-Fri 1030-1730, Sat 1030-1700, Sun 1300-1700, free*. One of the lesser-known galleries in the city, the RBSA has strong Pre-Raphaelite connections (Sir Edward Burne-Jones was a former president) and there's some spectacular locally designed jewellery for sale, too.

To find out whether diamonds really are a girl's best friend – or is it gold, silver, emeralds, rubies or sapphires – you can visit over 500 shops concentrated round **Vittoria Street**, Frederick Street and **Vyse Street** where you'll also find **The Museum of the Jewellery Quarter** ① *75-79, Vyse St, T0121-554 3598, www.bmag.org.uk, Tue-Sat 1030-1600, guided tour £5, concessions £4, under 16s free, free entry to temporary exhibitions*. The factory closed in 1981, the door was locked and everything was left as it was. Today, it gives an insight into Smith & Pepper's former business and tells the story of the Jewellery Quarter. The tour also includes a demonstration of jewellery-making techniques.

If you have time on your hands, the **Pen Museum** ① *Frederick St, T0121-236 9834, www.penroom.co.uk, Mon-Sat 1100-1600, Sun 1300-1600*, is a free museum showcasing one of Birmingham's forgotten bygone industries.

Hurst Street and around

One of Birmingham's key sites of regeneration, the city elders took a fairly ropey collection of old pubs and the Hippodrome theatre and turned it into one of the trendiest, safest and smartest areas the city has to offer. A fantastic pot-pourri of the **Chinese Quarter**, the gay district and The Arcadian development, this is definitely worth a visit if you're spending one night in Brum.

If you're interested in learning more about the people who used to live in the area, the National Trust runs the popular **Back to Backs tour** ① *T0121-666 7671, www.nationaltrust. org.uk, Tue-Sun 1000-1700, but during term time closed 1000-1300 Tue-Thu, last tour times vary in winter, closed 31 Aug-6 Sep*, which must be booked in advance. By visiting the houses, it takes you through from the 1840s to the 1970s, offering a glimpse of the lives of former residents.

The Barber Institute of Fine Arts

Though few can believe it, Birmingham really is incredibly green and just 15 minutes south of the city centre, you hit **Edgbaston**, supposedly Brum's poshest and leafiest suburb. Take the No 61 or 63 bus from Navigation Street down the Bristol Road (the continuation of Broad Street after Five Ways) and get off next to *The Gun Barrels* pub. The No 98 also leaves the city centre from Colmore Row, and stops on Edgbaston Park Road. If coming by train from New Street, University Station is a five minute walk from the Barber Institute.

The Barber Institute of Fine Arts ① *University of Birmingham, Edgbaston, B15 2TS, T0121-414 7333, www.barber.org.uk, Mon-Fri 1000-1700, Sat-Sun 11-1700, free*, houses a truly superlative collection of Old Masters with some stunning impressionists and modern pieces. The award-winning art deco building comes complete with a concert hall, modest café and a full programme of concerts and History of Art lectures.

Moseley and The Tolkien Trail

Though there's currently a battle royal underway between Oxford and Birmingham to claim JRR Tolkien as a native son, Brum has by far the better claim, as he was educated at King Edward's School and spent much of his childhood around Moseley and King's Heath. Moseley Village is an excellent place to start the Tolkien trail, perhaps in the smoke room of **The Prince of Wales** where the youthful JRR had secret assignations with his bride to be. From there, it's just a quick stagger down to Alcester Road where you can see a plaintive blue plaque commemorating the youthful Tolkien's residence. If you're requiring more refreshment as well as another stop on the Tolkien pilgrimage, the Weatherspoon's pub **The Elizabeth of York** in Moseley plays host to a sculpture commemorating *The Lord of the Rings* designed and built by the author's great-nephew Tim Tolkien. But the real Tolkien afficionados will want to make the mysterious journey down The Wake Green Road to **Sarehole Mill** ① *T0121-777 6612, Apr-Oct Tue-Fri 1300-1600, Sat-Sun 1200-1600, adults £3, concessions £2, under 16s free*, and the rather sinister-sounding **Moseley Bog**, which was undoubtedly the inspiration for Bilbo, Frodo and other assorted hobbits' beloved Shire. Tolkien loved this area and even in later life when he was living in posh North Oxford donated money to have Sarehole Mill restored. It's another of those perfectly restored living museums with a vistors' centre. Moseley Bog, on the other hand, is still in a wild state, carefully preserved as a virtually tourist-free zone.

Walsall and The Lickey Hills

So called because the grime and pollution turned every man, woman and child's face a darker shade of grey, **The Black Country**, which lies to the north of Birmingham, had been avoided by tourists for at least two centuries. But now there's an excellent reason for making a beeline for Walsall, which lies at its heart. **The New Art Gallery Walsall** ① *T01922-624 510, Gallery Sq, Walsall, WS2 8LG, www.thenewartgallerywalsall.org.uk, Tue-Sat 1000-1700, Sun 1200-1600, free*, is a stunning, award-winning £21 million building, housing a really superb collection, amassed by Jacob Epstein's widow and the daughter of an American industrial magnate. Once you're in Walsall you might as well visit **The Walsall Arboretum** ① *T01922-654 318, Lichfield St, daily, free*, a 19th-century pleasure garden with a boating lake. For more information on walks in the area, contact **Walsall Countryside Services** ① *T01922-459 813, countrysideservices@walsall.gov.uk*.

　　The Lickey Hills to the west of Birmingham City Centre and easily accessible on a 63 bus, only 15 minutes from town, are also a splendid country location where you can stretch your legs and see some wonderful flora and fauna.

Birmingham listings

For hotel and restaurant price codes and other relevant information, see pages 9-12.

● Where to stay

Birmingham *p18, map p20*

££££-£££ Hotel Du Vin, Church St, B3 2NR, T0844-736 4250. A fantastic conversion of the old eye hospital, this hotel also has a popular brasserie.

££££-£££ The Hyatt Regency, 2 Bridge St, B1 2JZ, T0121-643 1234, www.birmingham.regency.hyatt.com. Right next to the ICC, so it's popular with conference delegates but try not to let that put you off. It's also got a sauna, spa, gym and swimming pool.

££££-£££ Staying Cool Rotunda, 150 New St, B2 4PA, T0121-285 1290, www.stayingcool.com/birmingham. On the top 2 floors of the Rotunda, stylish serviced apartments with great views. Floor-to-ceiling windows, espresso machine and even oranges for the juicer.

£££ 52 and 54 Inge Street, B5 4TE, T0844-800 2070, www.nationaltrustcottages.co.uk. The National Trust rents out 2 of the cottages to visitors for a minimum of 1 night. One styled in the 1930s and one in the Victorian period. An atmospheric option.

£££ Jury's Inn, 245 Broad St, B1 2HQ, T0121-606 9000, www.birminghamhotels.jurysinns.com. A huge tower-block-like structure, right round the corner from the thriving melee of Broad St.

£££ Macdonald Burlington Hotel, 6 Burlington Arcade, 126 New St, B2 4JQ, T0844-879 9019, www.macdonaldhotels.co.uk. A good central option for those travelling by train, and you can tuck into a steak at the **Berlioz** restaurant.

£££ Plough and Harrow, 135 Hagley Rd, B16 8LS, T0121-454 4111, www.ploughandharrowhotel.co.uk. The poshest pub you're ever likely to spend the night in, without things such as swimming pools or saunas, but a beautiful, peaceful garden instead.

£££-££ Malmaison, The Mailbox, 1 Wharfside St, B1 1RD, T0844-693 0651, www.malmaison.com. Birmingham's **Malmaison** offering is in a converted Royal Mail Sorting Office. Good rooms, a restaurant and bar.

££-£ The Bloc Hotel St Paul's, Caroline St, B3 1UG, T0121-212 1223, www.blochotels.com. Tiny rooms in the heart of the Jewellery Quarter. Stylish, comfortable and reasonably priced, but think pod rather than hotel room.

££-£ Ibis, Ladywell Walk, B5 4ST, T0121-619 9000, www.ibis.com. Like other **Ibis** hotels it's short on decor but long on convenience, especially if you want to gorge yourself on Chinese food; it's in the heart of Brum's Chinatown.

£ Birmingham Central Backpackers, 58 Coventry St, Digbeth, B5 5NH, T0121-643 0033, www.birminghambackpackers.com. Walking distance from central sights and near the bus station. Friendly with a buzzing common room, offers free Wi-Fi and breakfast. Accommodation is in 2 adjoining buildings. Dorms and private rooms.

❼ Restaurants

Birmingham *p18, map p20*

£££ Purnell's, 55 Cornwall St, B3 2DH, T0121-212 9799, www.purnellsrestaurant.com. Glynn Purnell's Michelin-starred restaurant. Multi-course tasting menus with wines, and there's also a 3-course lunch offering. Modern, innovative food including dishes such as poached egg yolk with smoked haddock, curry oil and cornflakes.

£££ Simpsons Restaurant, 20 Highfield Rd, B15 3DU, T0121-454 3434, www.simpsonsrestaurant.co.uk. Another Michelin-starred restaurant, in what was once a Georgian mansion. Classic dishes with a Mediterranean twist. Set menus or à la carte. It is also home to a cookery school.

£££ Turners, 69 High St, Harborne, B17 9NS, T0121-426 4440, www.turnersrestaurant birmingham.co.uk. Busy neighbourhood restaurant and another Michelin star. Serves modern British cooking. Set evening and lunchtime menus, the Simply Turners ranges from 3 courses to 5.

£££-££ Bank, 4 Brindleyplace, B1 2JB, T0121-633 4466, www.individualrestaurants.com. Upmarket dining with a great view of the canals. Seasonal ingredients with dishes ranging from risotto to Thai green chicken curry. A wide range of steak cuts on offer.

£££-££ Cielo, 6 Oozells Sq, Brindleyplace, B1 2JB, T0121-632 6882. Italian fine dining. The lunchtime and early evening fixed menus are good value.

££ Anderson's Bar & Grill, 30 Mary Ann St, St Paul's Sq, B3 1RL, T0121-200 2515, www.andersonsbarandgrill.co.uk. In a converted silversmith's cellar, this was formerly known as **The Bucklemaker**. Serves predominantly steaks but there are other options, including a couple of veggie dishes, and an interesting tapas menu that includes Welsh rarebit.

££ Chung Ying Garden, 17 Thorp St, B5 4AT, T0121-666 6622, www.chungying.co.uk. Chinese restaurant in the heart of the Chinese district, with a family atmosphere and authentic feel.

££ Jamie's Italian, Middle Mall, Bullring Shopping Centre, T0121-270 3610, www.jamieoliver.com/italian. One of a number of chain restaurants at the Bullring. You're probably already familiar with the formula but there are pastas, burgers and fish dishes, as well as a range of sharing plates.

££ The Karczma, Polish Millennium House, Bordesley St, Digbeth, B5 5PH, T0121-448 0017. www.thekarczma.co.uk. Closed Mon. Ignore the less than inviting exterior and head inside for delicious and filling Polish food.

££ Le Truc, Ladywell Walk, The Arcadian, B5 4ST, T0121-622 7050, www.letruc.co.uk. French restaurant with friendly service, and great food. There's a specials board and a pre-theatre menu. Cocktails and a decent wine list.

££-£ Thai Edge, Six Brindleyplace, 7 Oozells St, B1 2HS, T0121-643 3993, www.thaiedge.co.uk. A really excellent Thai restaurant with stunning decor, and reasonably priced.

££-£ The Lost & Found, 8 Bennetts Hill, B2 5RS, T0121-643 9293, www.the-lostandfound.co.uk. British food or cocktails in bright and leafy surroundings, the Botanical Garden is reminiscent of a Victorian library. Come for a full English, a Sun roast or just a sandwich.

££-£ Minmin Noodle Bar, Unit 4 Latitude Building, Bromsgrove St, B5 6AB, T0121-622 5955. Family-run restaurant serving up delicious food made with fresh ingredients. Come for the huge noodle soups.

Curry houses

The large Pakistani and Kashmiri communities in Birmingham invented the Balti in the mid 1970s and there are still many of the café-style restaurants with glass-topped tables that appeal to Balti purists dotted around this area. The easiest way to get to the Balti Triangle is to go down the Moseley Rd (A435) or the Stratford Rd (A34). Both will take you to Sparkbrook and Balsall Heath where the best Balti houses are to be found, many of them on Ladypool Road dubbed 'the corridor of curry'. A few restaurants in the Triangle sell curry, some will let you BYO and some are dry.

£££-££ Lasan, 3-4 Dakota Buildings, B3 1SD, T0121-212 3664, www.lasan.co.uk. This restaurant won best local restaurant on Gordon Ramsay's *F Word* programme in 2010, and continues to serve innovative and delicious food.

££-£ Adil, 148 Stoney La, B12 8AJ, T0121-449 0335, www.adilbalti.co.uk. Allegedly this is where it all started – it's one of the oldest balti houses and possibly the best. Beware of the green chilli bhaji starter – not for the faint-hearted.

££-£ Deolali, 23A St Mary's Row, B13 8HW, T0121-442 2222, www.deolalirestaurant.com. One of the more 'upmarket' curry options with stylist interior. Complete with wine list, and modern and traditional dishes.

££-£ Kababish, 29 Woodbridge Rd, B13 8EH, T0121-449 5556, www.kababish.co.uk. If you're looking for a more upmarket balti experience than can be found in Sparkbrook, this is the place for you.

££-£ Maharajah, 23/25 Hurst St, B5 4AS, T0121-622 2641, www.maharajarestaurant. co.uk. Another contrast to the Balti Triangle, this is upmarket Indian as you've never tasted it before and is apparently patronized by the Indian cricket team when they're playing down the road at Edgbaston.

£ Shereen Kada, 543 Moseley Rd, B12 9BU, T0121-440 4641. If you're into sugar overloads then this is the place for you, as its reputation as an Indian sweet centre is unparalleled. The baltis are pretty good too.

🕜 Pubs, bars and clubs

Birmingham *p18, map p20*

The Bull's Head, St Mary's Row, Moseley, B13 8HW, T0121-702 0931, www.bullshead moseley.co.uk. One of the places to come for music, ranging from live gigs to club nights.

The Cross, 145 Alcester Rd, B13 8JP, T0121-449 6300, thecrossmoseley.com. Moseley's movers and shakers flock here, it has a great space out front for that boulevardier feeling.

Hare & Hounds, 106 High St, King's Heath, B14 7JZ, T0121-444 2081, www. hareandhoundskingsheath.co.uk. Sister venue of **The Bull's Head** (see above), this is a pub and live music venue, and is one of 'the' places to come to see new and established acts.

The Lord Clifden, 34 Great Hampton St, Hockley, B18 6AA, T0121-523 7515, www.thelordclifden.co.uk. A contemporary take on the tradition pub, with real ales and framed street art.

The Old Joint Stock, 4 Temple Rd West, B2 5NY, T0121-200 1892, www.oldjoint stocktheatre.co.uk. You can tell from the spectacular interior that this place used to be something very grand – in fact it was the Birmingham Stock Exchange. The pub shares the building with a theatre and is worth a visit, if only to see the domed ceiling. Sun lunchtime Jazz.

The Old Moseley Arms, 53 Tindall St, B12 9QU, T0121-440 1954. Despite being a down-home traditional boozer with excellent beer, this place has a nice mix of clientele.

The Prince of Wales, 118 Alcester Rd, Moseley, B13 8EE, T0121-449 4198, www.theprincemoseley.co.uk. Trendy bars come and go, but the PoW has been serving beer for generations. Under its new management it has been spruced up and now boasts a cocktail bar but it's still as good as it always was. Highly recommended.

The Tap and Spile, 16 Gas St, B1 2JT, T0121-632 5602, www.tapandspilebirmingham. co.uk. Here since 1821, this old-fashioned boozer that looks out over the canal and offers a superlative pint.

The Wellington, 37 Bennett's Hill, B2 5SN, T0121-200 3115, www.thewellingtonrealale. co.uk. A small pub offering a good range of real ales that change regularly. No food served, but bring your own and they'll supply the cutlery.

Clubs

Air, 49 Heath Mill Lane, T0121-766 6646, www.airbirmingham.com. This former warehouse is Brum's super-club. God's Kitchen events on Sat are the ones to go for.

The Jam House, 3-5 St Pauls Sq, B31QU, T0121-200 3030, www.thejamhouse.com/ birmingham. Popular with an older crowd, with great live music and a packed dance floor. You can book a table and eat here as well.

Nightingale, Essex House, Kent St, B5 6RD, T0121-622 1718, www.nightingaleclub. co.uk. A long-established and popular gay club catering to a range of music tastes.

The Rainbow, 160 High St, Digbeth, B12 0LD, www.therainbowvenues.co.uk. A laidback venue that attracts a mix of punters. Drinks, live music, DJs, it's all on offer here.

Birmingham *p18, map p20*

Cinema

Electric Cinema, 47-49 Station St, B5 4DY, T0121-643 7879, www.theelectric.co.uk. The UK's oldest working cinema. Grab a sofa, tuck into homemade cakes and catch up the mainstream and indie releases. Highly recommended.

Empire Cinemas, Great Park, Park Way, Rubery, B45 9JL, T0871-471 4714, www.empirecinemas.co.uk.

Giant Screen, Millennium Point, Curzon St, B4 7XG, T0121-202 2222, www.giantscreen cinema.co.uk. Does what it says on the tin, it offers a 72ft-wide cinema screen. Showing a couple of latest releases and 3D films.

Mac (Midlands Arts Centre), Cannon Hill Rd, B12 9QH, T0121-446 3232, www.macarts.co.uk. An intelligently programmed independent cinema.

Odeon, New St, T0871-224 4007, www.odeon.co.uk.

Vue, Unit 29, Star City, Watson Rd, Nechells, T0871-224 0240, www.myvue.com.

Music

For other live music venues, see Pubs, bars and clubs, page 28.

The Barber Institute of Fine Arts, University of Birmingham, Edgbaston, B15 2TS, Edgbaston Park Rd, T0121-414 7333, www.barber.org.uk. It's not only got a fantastic gallery, but there's also a concert hall which specializes in chamber music and small ensembles. Lunchtime and evening concerts.

NEC, M42, Junction 6, B40 1NT, T0121-780 4141, www.thenec.co.uk. For those who prefer their rock large, loud and epic, here's one of the original stadia for which the term stadium rock was invented. Not surprisingly, it's a personality-free zone.

NIA, King Edward's Rd, B1 2AA, T0121-780 4141, www.thenia.co.uk. It's owned by the same people who own the NEC, so it's got the same sort of character (ie none), but you can catch the B list acts there, as well as some stand-up comedy.

O2 Academy Birmingham Academy, 16-18 Horsefair, Bristol St, B1 1DB, T0844-477 2000, www.o2academybirmingham.co.uk. Gigs and club nights, well-known bands as well as those better-kept secrets are showcased.

Symphony Hall, Broad St, B1 2EA, T0121-345 0600, www.thsh.co.uk. One of the best, most acoustically perfect, purpose-built venues in the country, the regular home of the CBSO (City of Birmingham Symphony Orchestra) and almost worth a visit even without live music. But the real thing is an incomparable experience.

Theatre

Alexandra Theatre, Station St, B5 4DS, T0844-871 3011, www.alexandratheatre.org. uk. West End hits as well as local fare.

Birmingham Repertory Theatre, Centenary Sq, Broad St, T0121-245 2000, www. birmingham-rep.co.uk. Until the end of 2013, performances will be taking place in a variety of venues around the city. After that the REP will be moving back to its Centenary Square home and sharing it with the new library. A good programme of ancient and modern, this place offers the best, most thought-provoking theatre outside Stratford.

The Hippodrome, Hurst St, B5 4TB, T0844-338 7000, www.birminghamhippodrome. com. Hosts the Birmingham Royal Ballet and the Welsh National Opera when they're on tour. It's also got the facilities to stage the really big West End hits when they come to town.

Mac (Midlands Arts Centre), Cannon Hill Rd, B12 9QH, T0121-446 3232, www.macarts. co.uk. An eclectic mix of slightly more avant-garde theatre pieces and dance. Lots of activities on offer for children and young people. See also Cinema, above.

✹ Festivals

Birmingham *p18, map p20*
Birmingham hosts a number of annual festivals and the Visit Birmingham website is a good source of listings. Some are listed below:
Jul Birmingham International Jazz & Blues Festival. Jazz and Blues at venues around the city and beyond. Musicians come from far and wide to perform.
Sep Artsfest (1st weekend of Sep), www.artsfest.org.uk. Though this has a slightly worthy feel (on account of being arranged and paid for by Birmingham City Council), it is chock full of free events which include live performances by some of the city's Bhangra combos, Asian dub or house. There's also performance art and all the best other art the region has to offer.
Oct Ramadan and Diwali. The city has a vocal and active Asian community and they celebrate their festivals in style, often with fireworks, big park parties and delicious food.
Nov-Dec Frankfurt Christmas Market. The largest outdoor Christmas market in the country, this is a popular tourist attraction. Nearly 200 stalls set up last year, selling food, crafts and decorations.

⬥ Shopping

Birmingham *p18, map p20*
There are a number of options for shopping in Birmingham city centre but perhaps the best known is **The Bullring** where you'll find **Selfridges**, as well as a large number of high-end and high street chain stores. The designer fan will want to pop in to the wharfside's **The Mailbox**, whereas those more interested in independent ventures should head to the **Custard Factory** on Gibb St. There are also shopping opportunities around **New Street**, **Corporation Street**, **The Minories** (off Bull St), **High St** and **Martineau Square** (off Union Passage). Not forgetting the jewellery shops in The Jewellery Quarter, for more information, see page 23.

Markets

Markets of Birmingham, beside St Martin's in the Bullring, are justly famed for the diversity of goods at bargain prices. At the **Outdoor Market** you'll find clothes, fabrics, china, kitchenware and exotic fruit and veg for sale Tue-Sat. The **Indoor Markets** sell fish, meat and fresh produce and are open every day except Sun.

The Bullring **Rag Market**, www.ragmarket.com, is worth a visit. Open 4 days a week (Tue, Thu, Fri and Sat) the stalls here are famous for the wealth of fabrics on sale but there are also stalls offering vintage clothes and jewellery amongst other goods.

If you can, visit **Brecknells**, 23 Union St, B2 4SW, T0121-643 1986, which is a great speciality shop. It's a wonderful old-school milliner (hat shop) and every type of fancy ladies' hat you can imagine – from the Jackie Kennedy pillbox to the Philip Treacy leopard skin floppy number worn by Boy George – is on offer and the staff are charming.

◉ What to do

Birmingham *p18, map p20*
Cricket
Warwickshire Country Cricket Club, The County Ground, Edgbaston, B5 7QU, T0844-847 1902 (match tickets), www.edgbaston.com. One of the best grounds in the world, Edgbaston has seen its fair share of test triumphs and tragedies.

Football
Birmingham has always been football crazy, and the teams that inspire most insanity are: **Aston Villa**, Villa Park, Trinity Rd, B6 6HE, www.avfc.co.uk, which offers a behind the scenes tour (check website for dates); **Birmingham City FC**, St Andrew's Rd, B9 4NH, www.bcfc.com; and **West Bromwich Albion**, The Hawthorns, Halford La, B71 4LF, www.wba.co.uk.

Greyhound racing

Hall Green Dog Track, Hall Green, B28 8LQ, T0870-840 8502, www.lovethedogs.co.uk. Admission £6. Racing on Fri and Sat night at 1930.

Karting

Grand Prix Karting, Adderley Rd South, B8 1AD, T0121-327 7700, www.grandprixkarting.co.uk. Outdoor circuits, karting from Tue to Sun. Must be booked in advance. Pricey but a lot of fun.

Tours

Back to Backs tour, see page 24.
Birmingham Tours, 134 Greenfield Rd, Harborne, B17 OEG, T0121-427 2555, www.birmingham-tours.co.uk. Offers a number of walking and driving tours of Birmingham, including a Tolkien bus tour. Tours need to be booked in advance.

Directory

Birmingham *p18, map p20*
Medical services Birmingham Children's Hospital, Steelhouse Lane, B4 6NH, T0121-333 9999. Birmingham Heartland's Hospital, Bordesley Green East, B9 5SS, T0121-424 2000. **City Hospital**, Dudley Rd, B18 7QH, T0121-554 3801. Has A&E. **NHS Medical Walk-in Centre**, Lower Ground Floor, Boots, 66 High St, B4 7TA, T0121-255 4500. Open daily. **Queen Elizabeth Hospital**, Edgbaston, B15 2TH, T0121-627 2000. Has A&E. **Police** Police Headquarters, Lloyd House, Colmore Circus, Queensway, B4 6NQ, T0845-113 5000. Digbeth Police Station, 113 Digbeth, B5 6DT, T0845-113 5000.
Post office 1 Pinfold St, T0845-722 3344.

Warwickshire

A mixed-up county in the southeastern shadow of Britain's second city, Warwickshire more than holds its own in the face of metropolitan Birmingham. Directly south, at Stratford-upon-Avon, the Bard is all around and theatrical performances of Shakespeare's plays reach new heights. Further east, Royal Leamington Spa repays a visit for its antique tone and thriving student scene keeping it awake at night. The university and county town of Warwick is next door, its much-publicized castle easily the star attraction. Warwick Castle, run by Madame Tussaud's, makes a terrifically entertaining and tourist-friendly meal of its fairytale architecture and bumpy history. Its less-hyped neighbour, Kenilworth, has even more extraordinary tales to tell about its crumbling ruins. Just to the north, the city of Coventry makes a much less obvious tourist destination. With its two extraordinary cathedrals and civic pride in the school of hard knocks it may say more about contemporary life in the Midlands than all the rest put together.

Stratford-upon-Avon → For listings, see pages 42-48.

As the world centre of an ever-expanding Shakespeare industry and Britain's second-most visited tourist destination after London, you would naturally expect there to be a preponderance of bard-related attractions in and around Stratford, but the place has nevertheless still managed to hold onto its authentic market-town atmosphere. The Royal Shakespeare Company is one of the artistic triumphs of the United Kingdom, and no visit to Stratford is really complete without seeing some of Shakespeare's drama – the play really is the thing in comparison with the Birthplace Trust Shakespeare trail. But if you haven't got enough time, and you still want to do the 'Willgrimage', you might drop in on Shakespeare's birthplace which has a tolerable exhibition, or see where Shakespeare was buried in Holy Trinity Church. As for the locals, they live in peace with the bard's sometimes troublesome legacy.

Arriving in Stratford-upon-Avon
Getting there As far as **trains** are concerned, there's an embarrassment of riches including a steam service, the **Shakespeare Express** ① *T0121-707 4696, www.shakespeareexpress. com, Jul-Sep Sun only*, which runs from Birmingham's Snow Hill station. **Chiltern Railways** go from London and Birmingham regularly and offer discounts for flexible travel in the region with the 'Shakespeare Explorer' ticket.

The M40 provides a speedy driving route for those coming from the north or south. Simply take exit 15 onto the A46, where Stratford is clearly signposted. If you prefer a more picturesque route from the south, there's the A3400 from Oxford, which will take you straight into Stratford town centre via some delightful Cotswolds towns such as Shipston on Stour (see below). From the southwest and the M5, take exit 9 at Tewkesbury and the A46 to Evesham (see below), then follow the signposts to Stratford. There's plenty of parking in Stratford.

Getting around Open-top sightseeing buses link Shakespeare's Birthplace, Anne Hathaway's Cottage and Hall's Croft and depart from the Visitor Information Centre on Bridgefoot.

Information The official **Visitor Information Centre** ① *Bridgefoot, T01789-264293, Mar-Oct daily 0900-1730, Nov-Feb Mon-Sat 0900-1730, Sun 1000-1600*, is by the Bridgefoot car park on one of the main routes in to Stratford-upon-Avon. This new, larger visitor centre has expanded to offer tickets, information, accommodation booking, internet and Skype services and a café.

Places in Stratford-upon-Avon
From the tourist office and Art Gallery see above, it's very easy to get to Stratford's main raison d'être: the **Royal Shakespeare Theatre**, towering over the landscape like an art deco power station. In fact it's quite a complex set of buildings, carefully designed to serve the great god Thespus with a varied platter. Also nestling within the arms of this great beast is a more delicate flower, the **Swan Theatre**, which now shares its front-of-house space with the Royal Shakespeare Theatre.

As befits such a dramatic place, the theatre has a chequered history including fire, passion and suicide. The present building was designed by Elizabeth Scott and was opened in 1932, but the original theatre on this site dates back to 1879 when a local brewer Edward Flower donated the land for the building. It was extensively renovated in 2010. For a fascinating insight, you can take a **behind the scenes tour** ① *T0844-800 1110, www.rsc.org.uk*; visit the RSC's **free exhibitions**, or climb the **Theatre Tower** ① *daily*

Stratford-upon-Avon

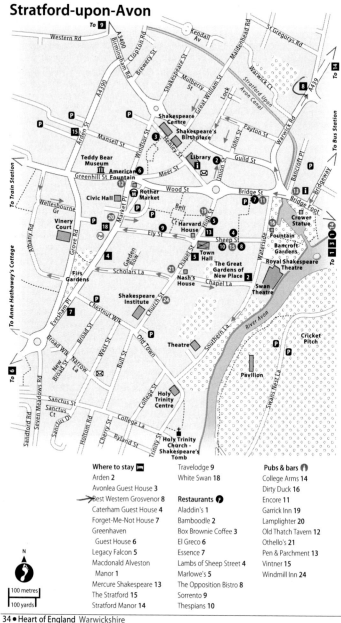

Where to stay 🛏
Arden 2
Avonlea Guest House 3
Best Western Grosvenor 8
Caterham Guest House 4
Forget-Me-Not House 7
Greenhaven
  Guest House 6
Legacy Falcon 5
Macdonald Alveston
  Manor 1
Mercure Shakespeare 13
The Stratford 15
Stratford Manor 14

Travelodge 9
White Swan 18

Restaurants 🍴
Aladdin's 1
Bamboodle 2
Box Brownie Coffee 3
El Greco 6
Essence 7
Lambs of Sheep Street 4
Marlowe's 5
The Opposition Bistro 8
Sorrento 9
Thespians 10

Pubs & bars 🍺
College Arms 14
Dirty Duck 16
Encore 11
Garrick Inn 19
Lamplighter 20
Old Thatch Tavern 12
Othello's 21
Pen & Parchment 13
Vintner 15
Windmill Inn 24

1000-1600, £2.50, children £1.25. Over 400 members of staff make scenery and costumes, maintain the theatre and administer its business.

Your most likely next port of call will be the collection of buildings run by the **Shakespeare's Birthplace Trust** ① *The Shakespeare Centre, Henley St, T01789-204016, www.shakespeare.org.uk, ticket for 5 properties £21.50, children £13.50, concessions £19.50, family £56 (valid for 1 year); other tickets also available.* The Shakespeare Centre is easily the most informative of the properties. There is a quite formidable team of Shakespeare scholars working with the Birthplace Trust, and a reading room which draws academics from round the world to look at this unique collection of first editions, history and scholarship. The centre can genuinely claim to be a site of world heritage. **Shakespeare's Birthplace** ① *Nov-Mar daily 1000-1600, Apr-Oct daily 1000-1700 (Jul and Aug until 1800),* also on Henley Street, is the jewel in the crown of the Shakespeare Properties. Even if there are a few gaps in our knowledge of Will's life (just who was the Dark Lady?), the Birthplace Trust are determined to do Will proud with this shrine to the man and the place that shaped his early life. A five-minute walk away on Chapel Lane is **Nash's House & New Place** ① *Nov-Mar daily 1100-1600, Apr-Oct daily 1000-1700,* a well-preserved Tudor House that was home to Shakespeare's granddaughter, and the site of Shakespeare's final home, which has been excavated; its archaeological treasures are on show. Another five-minute walk to Old Town takes you to **Hall's Croft** ① *Nov-Mar daily 1000-1600, Apr-Oct daily 1000-1700,* the elegant Jacobean home of Shakespeare's daughter, Susanna, which display the intriguing apothecary equipment of her husband, a doctor. 2013 is the 400th anniversary of this property. Two miles west of the town is **Anne Hathaway's Cottage** ① *Shottery, Nov-Mar daily 1000-1600, Apr-Oct daily 0900-1700,* easily reached by car or a pleasant 30-minute walk. This is the second-most visited of the Shakespeare Properties and really is exquisitely maintained, with original furniture and the most beautiful gardens. Finally, three miles north of the city is **Mary Arden's Farm** ① *Wilmcote, Apr-Oct daily 1000-1700,* which was Shakespeare's mother's home. This property offers the experience of an authentic working Tudor farm, and 2013 is its 500th anniversary. Wilmcote railway station is just opposite the farm, or there is parking available.

In complete contrast, there's **Falstaff's Experience/Tudor World** ① *40 Sheep St, T01789-298070, www.falstaffexperience.co.uk, Mon-Sat 1030-1730, £6, children £3, concessions £4.50,* a gimmicky place that tries to bring Shakespeare's world to life by the power of animatronics and weird smells in one of the most historical properties in Stratford. It's probably a bit more immediate and tangible for kids than a five-hour session in the theatre watching the Dane play out his terrible fate, but one can't help feeling these operations somehow cheapen history. Ghost tours also available.

Next, pay a visit to the **MAD Museum** (Mechanical, Art and Design Museum) ① *Sheep St, T01789-269356, www.themadmuseum.co.uk, Oct-Mar daily 1100-1700, Apr-Sep daily 1030-1830, £6.80, children £4.50, concessions £5.50, family £19,* a small but fascinating museum displaying machines and mechanical paraphernalia, art, contraptions and gizmos.

Rejoining the Shakespeare Trail should now be your top priority. **Holy Trinity Church** ① *Old Town Stratford, T01789-266316, www.stratford-upon-avon.org, Mar and Oct Mon-Sat 0900-1700, Sun 1230-1700; Apr-Sep Mon-Sat 0830-1800, Sun 1230-1700; Oct-Feb Mon-Sat 0900-1600, Sun 1230-1700, Shakespeare's Grave £2, children £1, students 50p,* is well worth the entrance fee. Seeing Shakespeare's tomb and monument isn't the only reason for visiting. The church is right next to the River Avon, and its setting and distinguished architecture give it a justifiable claim to be one of England's loveliest parish churches.

Another great way to spend some time is by following the **River Avon Trail**, a great place to stroll or cycle through the town to the west, with great views of the theatre and thatched cottages.

Leamington Spa and around → *For listings, see pages 42-48.*

Royal Leamington Spa

The most magnificent example of Royal Leamington Spa's heyday is the **Royal Pump Rooms**, first opened in 1811, and to this day the elegant heart of this miniature Regency town. Certainly the poor relation of Bath and Cheltenham, Leamington was nevertheless granted a royal charter by Victoria in 1838. Anxious to shake off the somewhat sad and decaying but genteel retirement atmosphere perfectly illustrated in John Betjeman's poem 'Death in Leamington', the place does have something to offer. With its nearby large student population from Warwick University, the town now has a reputation for unruly partying on its main streets, and out of term-time and during the week, Leamington is a charming treasure trove of distinguished architecture, pleasant walks and upmarket eateries.

Around Leamington

There are a profusion of delightful south Warwickshire villages to visit nearby, many of which have great walks and opportunities for wining and dining as well as the odd spectacular view, the best of which can probably be found in **Ufton**, on the A425 Daventry Road between Leamington Spa and Southam, about four miles from Leamington, where there's also a **Nature Reserve**. The village pub is called *The White Hart* (signed from the main road). It has a good reputation for food and a beer garden with a good view over rolling countryside. Another great pub in a gem of a village is the **Fleur De Lys** at **Lowsonford**, right next to the **Stratford Canal**. Other excellent villages rejoice in names such as **Bishop's Itchington**.

Warwick and Kenilworth → *For listings, see pages 42-48.*

Warwick and its environs is really a tale of two castles. One is a romantic ruin and the other is a ruined opportunity. Between them, Kenilworth and Warwick Castles dominate this part of the world and have done for centuries. From medieval pageants to pitched battles, the castles are a fantastic double act. As always, it's the powerful elite who really grab our interest in the history of this little and fairly quiet town, the county capital of Warwickshire. Throughout history, royals couldn't keep away from the place, so it's not surprising that the local population have developed a habit of turning a blind eye to the more outlandish excesses of visitors. Since Warwick Castle still employs many local people – just as it used to when it needed an army of servants to satisfy the whims of its pampered weekenders – the locals have learnt the value of discretion. This all leads to a very pleasant atmosphere – intensely peaceful, although some might find it a mite too stately for their tastes. Never mind, if you want nightclubs, go to Leamington. If you want superb slices of history, vividly portrayed and well preserved, however, stick to Warwick and Kenilworth.

Arriving in Warwick

Getting there Warwick train station is 10 minutes' **walk** from the town centre and castle. Regular **trains** run from Birmingham on the Chiltern Line which can be picked up in London from Marylebone Station. Use Leamington Spa for connections to Banbury, Coventry and Oxford. The best way to approach Warwick from the north is either via the M1, taking the M69 and A46, or M6 taking the M42 to M40 junction 15, then A429 to Warwick. From London also use the M40 to junction 15 then A429 to Warwick.

Information Warwick's **main Tourist Office** ⓘ *Jury St, T01926-492212, www.visitwarwick. co.uk,* is within easy striking distance of the castle and most other attractions.

Warwick Castle

ⓘ *CV34 4QU, T01926-495421, www.warwick-castle.com (also for information on all events held at the castle), open from 1000 but check website for closing times, which vary throughout the year, and prices (cheaper if booked in advance).*

Admittedly Warwick Castle seems to be a classic tourist trap. It's full of live archers, waxwork tableaux and living exhibits which are all the trademarks of the 'heritage industry' – in this case Tussaud's, its most successful beneficiary and the owners since 1978. Actually Tussaud's have done a rather good job and they spent over £20 million restoring the castle from a fairly parlous state.

Warwick Castle is now a major site of historic interest and it's not only an incredible structure – a proper medieval fort – but it was also an icon of taste and style for the upper classes of the past four centuries. Canaletto immortalized several famous prospects and even JMW Turner couldn't resist its perfect lines and fairy-tale romanticism. The real money shots, however, are to be found above the castle – where you can see the outlines of the original earthworks which Aethelwade built to defend herself over 1000 years ago.

Tussaud's come into their own, though, once you enter the castle through the magnificent **Gatehouse** and **Barbican**. The main precinct enclosed by the east and south walls is in tip-top condition with an immaculate lawn sometimes used for torchlit feasts. Immediately, you are surrounded by the walls and battlements of an honest-to-goodness fairy-tale castle.

Assuming you're going to leave a stroll around the **towers and ramparts** for later, a good place to start your tour is at **Kingmaker: Eve of Battle**, commemorating the almost total power one Earl of Warwick, Richard Neville, enjoyed over the kingdom.

Just around the corner from Kingmaker, there's the **Chapel, Great Hall and State Rooms**, where you'll find the Warwicks' fairly large collection of antiques, gorgeous furniture and slightly boring portraits. There are things in these rooms that betray a certain lack of taste and borderline vulgarity, especially the **Blue Boudoir** which is powder blue and very camp. There is, however, a superb school of Holbein portrait of Henry VIII looking very macho. But the magic of waxworks really comes into its own in the adjacent rooms to the chapel and state rooms which are occupied by **The Royal Weekend Party** a faithful reconstruction of a house party held in 1898 at which two future kings were present as guests. But the holy of holies in this sequence is undoubtedly **The Kenilworth Bedroom**, a room set aside permanently for the Prince of Wales because he was such a frequent visitor.

As you'd expect the grounds are immaculate and absolutely litter free; showing off some spectacular features such as the **Victorian Rose Garden** and the **Pageant Field** as well as the **Peacock Garden** designed by 19th-century landscapist Robert Warnock. There's also a truly fabulous **Conservatory** designed in 1786 to house the famous **Warwick Vase** an enormous piece of Roman pottery gifted to an 18th-century Earl in recognition of his diplomatic skills.

Additional sights, not included in the main ticket are **The Dragon Tower**, a walk-through Arthurian show inspired by the BBC programme *Merlin* and **The Castle Dungeon**, where actors bring the gruesome history of the castle to life. It really is scary and not suitable for young children. These experiences work on a timed ticket system and can be bought on the day or in advance online.

Kenilworth Castle

ⓘ *(EH), T01926-852078, CV8 1NE, www.english-heritage.org.uk, see website for opening times, £8.20, child £4.90, concessions £7.40, family £21.30. By car: at M6 junction (M42 Junction 7) take A452 south into Kenilworth. From Coventry and Warwick, Kenilworth is off the A46 on the A452 and the castle is signposted from the town centre; parking charges apply. By train: Coventry Station is 8 miles. By bus: Stagecoach X17 and 16 from Coventry, Leamington Spa and Warwick. A free shuttle bus runs from the town centre 1000-1800.*

In many ways, Kenilworth Castle has more history to offer than Warwick as its bloody story has witnessed savagery, skulduggery and at one point it even played its part in regicide. But unlike Warwick Castle it's an honest-to-goodness ruin, a fact not lost on its most famous chronicler, Sir Walter Scott, whose novel of 1821 describing the spectacular culmination of an alleged love-affair between Elizabeth I and Robert Dudley, Earl of Leicester, really put Kenilworth on the tourist map and helped to draw crowds wanting to experience the romance of an ancient ruin first-hand. Dickens used to pay frequent visits and more recently, the Castle has helped inspire modern fabulists obsessed by the medieval and spooky – JRR Tolkien and JK Rowling to name but two.

The current structure was begun in around 1120 by Geoffrey De Clinton, a counter-jumping Chamberlain to Henry I. De Clinton's formidable grasp of warcraft can be seen in the mighty Norman stone keep called **Caesar's Tower**, built in the style of a Roman fort – very high and very square, with walls that are over 20ft thick. De Clinton also thoughtfully encircled his stronghold with water – the largest artificial lake in the kingdom at that time. It was this feature, along with **The Curtain Walls** surrounding the castle which King John later built, that helped the structure withstand a nine-month siege and every type of military onslaught when in 1266, Henry III tried to put a stop to the current castle-keeper Simon De Montfort's campaign to curb the power of the monarchy in the wake of the Magna Carta (1215).

De Montfort had started the process of turning the castle into a palace and centre of scholarship and when Henry III took it over and gave it to his son Edmund Earl of Lancaster later to become Earl of Leicester; it was one of the five licensed jousting and royal tournament centres in the kingdom. In celebration of the defeat of the Barons, a splendid gathering of over 100 knights, known as 'the round table' took place at Kenilworth in 1279 and all kinds of noble revelry, including jousting was staged in **The Tiltyard**, a purpose-built gaming and tournament field which can still be visited.

The castle passed ultimately to John of Gaunt, a medieval 'Godfather' figure who as son of Edward III became de facto king on the accession of Richard II who was only twelve at the time. His influence can be seen everywhere, but particularly in the remains of **The Great Hall** to the left of the **Keep**.

But the beautification of Kenilworth reached its apotheosis under Robert Dudley, Earl of Leicester who wanted to impress his royal patron (and possibly mistress) with the most incredible reception and party which lasted 19 days in 1575. He even built a special tower **The Leicester Building** for the Queen and her retinue as well as a new triumphal entrance to the castle, **Leicester's Gatehouse**. The private garden he created for the queen was recreated in as authentic a manner as possible and reopened to the public in 2009 as the **Elizabethan Garden**.

Other sights around Warwick

Baddesley Clinton ① *(NT), 6 miles northwest of Warwick off A4141, Rising Lane, B93 0DQ, T01564-783294, www.nationaltrust.org.uk, check website for opening times,* made its name as a haven for Catholics and it contains three priest holes secreted about its beautiful structure, which is an outstanding example of a moated manor house dating back to the 15th century.

But for real fans of exquisite interiors, there's peerless **Packwood House** ① *(NT), 10 miles northwest of Warwick, Packwood La, Lapworth, B94 6AT, T01564-782024, www.nationaltrust.org.uk, check website for opening times,* a building first lived in in the 16th century. Famed designer Graham Baron Ash got his hands on it in the interwar period in the 20th century and he turned it into one of the smartest country houses in Britain, but cleverly preserved its connection with the past by decorating it with 16th-century period textiles and furniture. The gardens are also a marvel and are known for their herbaceous borders and yew trees.

Coventry → *For listings, see pages 42-48.*

The paradox of Coventry is that it's one of the oldest towns in the country but has one of the newest centres. There were Anglo-Saxon settlers arriving before AD900, but thanks to Hitler and his first most devastating bombing raid in November 1940, only fragments of Old Coventry remain. So there's a decidedly 1970s' urban concrete nightmare feel to some of it, and this, combined with Coventry's reputation in recent years as a bit of a rough place, has made it distinctly unappetizing for the average tourist. Of course, the reason Coventry was targeted by the Nazi bombing raids in the first place was because it was an important industrial centre, especially for the automotive industries, who are still big employers in the area, so you wouldn't necessarily expect it to be all medieval mews and grassy banks. And it's this big difference between Coventry and its near neighbours Stratford and Warwick that you should bear in mind when visiting – it's a proper working city. That's not to say that it hasn't got its fair share of magical history – the Lady Godiva story alone would be enough to guarantee it a place in the pantheon of British folklore, quite apart from the fact that the story benefits from being largely true. And right in the middle of the Cathedral precinct, next door to one another, are the perfect symbols of Coventry's past and present: the old and new Cathedrals. The modern one is a masterpiece.

Arriving in Coventry

Getting there Trains are every 20 minutes from London Euston or Birmingham on **Virgin Trains** ① *www.virgintrains.co.uk, less frequent on Sun.* From London M1, Junction 17, take the M45 which become the A45 at Thurlaston for the south side of the city. Or take the M1 to Junction 19, then the M6 to Junction 2 and then the A4600 for the northeast of the city. From the north take the M1 to Junction 21 and the M69 to Junction 2 and then the A4600, or the M6 the Junction 3 and then the A444. **National Express** ① *www.nationalexpress.com,* runs buses to Coventry from around the country.

Getting around Most places that you would want to see in the centre of Coventry are accessible on foot, but you will probably need to catch a bus from the station to the Cathedral or it's about a 15-minute walk. **Allens Taxis** ① *T0247-655 5555.* For further information on getting around this part of the country, see www.networkwestmidlands.com.

Two Tone Town

Racially diverse youth culture has always been in evidence in this big-city melting pot. And it was this ethnic stew which led in the late 70s and early 80s to the emergence of a genuinely important youth movement which had its own distinctive sound: Two Tone. Even its name reflects the euphoric moment when black and white kids got together to make great tunes in the same bands, the best of which was The Specials who were originally called 'The Coventry Specials'. Their seminal Ghost Town was about Coventry, its sad concrete wastelands featuring extensively in a rare early example of the pop video which was released to accompany the song. Sadly the Tic Toc Club where it all started is no longer standing, but if you really want to hear the ghosts of Jerry Dammers et al, you can still get close to the original site.

Nowadays, Coventry's biggest connection with youth culture and especially music is genius pop entrepreneur Pete Waterman, the man who gave us Kylie, a whole host of other mega success stories and, er, Jason Donovan.

Information The city centre **tourist office** ① *Cathedral Ruins, Priory St, CV1 5AB, T024-7622 5616, www.visitcoventryandwarwickshire.co.uk, tower climb £2.50, child £1*, is in St Michael's Tower. In the summer you can climb the 180 steps and enjoy the panorama from the top.

Places in Coventry

Holy Trinity Church ① *5a Priory Row, CV1 5EX, T024-7622 0418, www.holytrinitycoventry. org.uk*, is notable for containing three styles of English Gothic and some very lovely stained glass. Its spire and tower collapsed in 1666 killing a passer-by, but was rebuilt even higher (237 ft). To its left is the sunken green of the **Priory Visitor's Centre** ① *Priory Walk, CV1 5EX, T024-7655 2242, www.prioryvisitorcentre.org, Mon-Sat 1000-1600, free*, where you can learn more about Coventry's first cathedral, the priory and the buildings' history. Exhibits include a glass painting of a woman's face, perhaps Lady Godiva as she has flowing wavy hair.

Coventry Cathedral ① *main entrance off Priory St, T024-7652 1200, www.coventrycathedral. org.uk*, is truly wonderful, an awe-inspiring place filled with many beautiful things. After the bombing of the old cathedral of St Michael's on 14th November 1940, Sir Basil Spence was charged with creating a suitable memorial to an ancient city which had suffered terribly in the Second World War. What he delivered between 1956 and 1962 was one of the most striking high-modernist buildings this side of Le Corbusier.

Some of the wonders on display include Epstein's sculpture outside the Cathedral of St Michael vanquishing the devil; *Christ Crucified*, a sculpture made from the metal of a wrecked motor car by Helen Jennings; John Piper's stained-glass Baptistry window; and also the engraved glass screen, *Saints and Angels*, by John Hutton, which is a particular highlight. The tiny Gethsemone Chapel displays a mosaic of the *Angel of Agony* (by Steven Sykes) seen through a beautifully designed crown of thorns (by Basil Spence). Graham Sutherland's tapestry above the altar, *Christ in Glory*, isn't to everyone's taste, but it's still an impressive sight dominating the east end of the nave.

In the remains of the **old Cathedral**, which has the eerie beauty of a living ruin, is Epstein's *Ecce Homo* and the statue *Reconciliation*, two figures embracing in sadness, an identical one is in the Peace Garden in Hiroshima. The statue was made by Josefina De Vasconcelos when she was 90 and was given to the Cathedral in 1995 by Richard Branson.

Leaving the Cathedral from the East end and turning right you come to the **Herbert Museum and Art Gallery** ① *Jordan Well, CV1 5QP, T0247-683 2386, www.theherbert. org, Mon-Sat 1000-1600, Sun 1200-1600, free*, which houses a selection of permanent collections as well as hosting temporary exhibitions. Upstairs there are a clutch of wonderful sculptures, a Henry Moore and Barbara Hepworth, for instance. And there's a whole room devoted to the famous story of **Lady Godiva**, who founded a famous Abbey in Coventry. But she's probably more famous as the wife of a local nobleman, Leofric, who was known for his cruel taxes. She appealed on behalf of the people of Coventry and he agreed to relent only if she rode naked through the city, which obligingly she did. It is said that only one citizen shamed himself by looking at her, a young man called Thomas and for ever after, the name *Peeping Tom* has been synonymous with sleazy voyeurism.

Also nearby is **St Mary's Guildhall** ① *Bayley Lane, CV1 5RN, T024-7683 3328, www. stmarysguildhall.co.uk, check the website for opening times*, which was originally built between 1340 and 1460, and restored in the 19th century. Inside are exhibited weapons, furniture and paintings but the real reason to visit is to see the medieval stained glass and because of its connection with Mary Queen of Scots, who was held here for a few months.

You can also get a feel for ancient Coventry at **Spon Street**, a partially reconstructed replica of an honest-to-goodness medieval street. The area lay outside the city walls along the banks of the river Sherborne which is now mostly underground. It was here that the noxiously stinky trades such as the tanning of hides and various other processes connected with wool were carried out. Today, the street is home to a number of shops, pubs and restaurants.

Coventry Transport Museum ① *Millennium Place, Hales St, CV1 1JD, T024-7623 4270, www.transport-museum.com, 1000-1700, free*, has the largest collection of British-made vehicles in the world, illustrating the development of transport from the bicycle to the jet engine. There are also normally events and temporary exhibitions, a recent one was British scooters of the 1960s and 70s.

Warwickshire listings

For hotel and restaurant price codes and other relevant information, see pages 9-12.

😑 Where to stay

Stratford-upon-Avon *p33, map p34*

££££ The Arden Hotel, Waterside, T01789-298682, www.theardenhotelstratford.com. An elegant and sophisticated hotel following its multi-million pound refurbishment. Directly opposite the Royal Shakespeare Theatres.

££££ The Legacy Falcon, Chapel St, T00844-411 9005, www.legacy-hotels.co.uk. A very comfortable, pleasant and historical hotel with a cosy bar and lounge.

££££ Macdonald Alveston Manor, Clopton Bridge, on the way out of the town on the Oxford Rd, T0844-879 9138, www.macdonaldhotels.co.uk. One of the finest hotels in Stratford, it enjoys a spectacular view of the river, has its own grounds and is within walking distance of the theatre.

£££ Best Western Grosvenor Hotel, Warwick Rd, T0845-776 7676. A nice example of this hotel chain, located in a Grade II-listed building.

£££ Mercure Shakespeare Hotel, Chapel St, T01789-294997, www.mercure.com. Grade I-listed Tudor building in a central location. Has a good lounge area and a cosy atmosphere and promises luxurious accommodation a stone's throw from all the town's attractions.

£££ The Stratford, Arden St, T01789-271000, www.qhotels.co.uk. A handsome Victorian townhouse that has been refurbished into a superior boutique hotel.

£££ Stratford Manor, Warwick Rd, T01789-731173, www.qhotels.co.uk. A very tidy, modern building, set in 21 acres of grounds, with a spa.

£££ The White Swan, Rother St, T01789-297022, www.white-swan-stratford.co.uk. Stylish and historic, this recently renovated hotel has some truly stunning rooms.

£££-££ Caterham Guest House, 58/59 Rother St, T01789-267309, www.caterhamhousehotel.co.uk. Individual character rooms in the heart of Stratford.

££ Avonlea Guest House, 47 Shipston Rd, T01789-205940, www.avonlea-stratford.co.uk. Under new ownership since 2011, this B&B offers modern, stylish and comfortable guest rooms.

££ Greenhaven Guest House, 217 Evesham Rd, T01789-294874. Pleasant, modern rooms in a 4-star guesthouse.

£ Forget-Me-Not Guest House, 18 Evesham Pl, T01789-204907, www.forgetmenotguesthouse.co.uk. With 5 en-suite rooms, this comfortable, cosy guesthouse is a bargain.

£ Travelodge Stratford-upon-Avon, 251 Birmingham Rd, T0871-984 6414. A basic but very affordable hotel a mile away from the city centre.

Self-catering

41 & 42 Shakespeare St, T01789-298141. £650 per week high season, £250 in low season. Two 3-bed apartments within easy walking distance of the centre. With off-street parking.

Lysander Court, Ely St, T01789-730275. This central townhouse accommodates 2-4 people. Minimum 2-night stay.

Caravans and camping

Riverside Park, Tiddington Rd, T01789-292313, www.stratfordcaravans.co.uk. This accommodation park offers fantastic 'snugs' – the wooden equivalent to tents – situated in a meadow overlooking the river, as well as standard caravans and lodges. Open Mar-Nov. No tents.

Leamington Spa *p36*

Leamington has an elegant sufficiency of hotels, B&Bs and inns, though what the tourist people like to call 'Shakespeare Country' has a much wider range.

££££ Mallory Court, Harbury Lane, just outside Leamington Spa, CV33 9QB, T01926-330214, www.mallory.co.uk. Manor house hotel with good food, check website for special offers.

£££-££ The Adams, Avenue Rd, CV31 3PQ, T01926-450742, www.adams-hotel.co.uk. Close to the centre and railway station. Small hotel offering good rooms, modern amenities and a delicious breakfast. Recommended.

££ The Angel Hotel, 143 Regent St, CV32 4NZ, T01926-881296, www.angel hotelleamington.co.uk. Central, friendly hotel with basic but clean rooms.

££ The Charnwood Guesthouse, 47 Avenue Rd, CV31 3PF, T01926-831074, www.charnwoodguesthouse.com.

££ The Premier Inn, Regency Arcade, The Parade, CV32 4BQ, T0871-527 9380, www.premierinn.com. Basic but reasonably priced chain hotel option, very central.

Warwick p36

££ Austin House Guest House, 96 Emscote Rd, T01926-493583, www.austinguesthouse.co.uk. Perfectly acceptable guesthouse in the guesthouse ghetto of Warwick.

££ Charter House, 87-91 West St, CV34 6AH, T01926-496965. Benefits from a great deal of privacy and a lovely garden. Serves great breakfasts. Recommended.

££ The Rose and Crown, 30 Market Pl, CV34 4SH, T01926-411117, www.roseandcrown warwick.co.uk. A former coaching inn, this pub now offers a small number of rooms above the pub. Very central but can be noisy.

££ The Seven Stars, 50 Friar St, CV37 6HD, T01926-492658, www.sevenstarswarwick.co.uk. Jolly inn-style establishment, enjoys patronage of locals. Highly recommended.

Coventry p39

If you need to stay the night here, it's worth looking outside the centre of the city. There are a number of Premier Inn hotels in the surrounding area.

££££-£££ The Coombe Abbey Hotel, Brinklow Rd, Binley, CV3 2AB, T0247-645 0450, www.coombeabbey.com. The site of the old Abbey where Elizabeth daughter of James I was imprisoned during the Gunpowder Plot. Superb grounds and facilities, a little way out of Coventry with award-winning dining.

££££-£££ The Hilton, Paradise Way, Walsgrave Triangle, CV2 2ST, T0247-660 3000, www.hilton.com. Luxurious inner city accommodation popular with business travellers.

££££-£££ Mercure Brandon Hall Hotel, Main St, Brandon, CV8 3FW, T0247-654 6000, www.accorhotels.com. Former shooting lodge in extensive grounds.

£££ MacDonald Ansty Hall Hotel, Main Rd, Ansty, CV7 9HZ, T0844-879 9031, www.macdonaldhotels.co.uk. 10 mins from the city centre, this is a 17th-century building which serves delicious food.

£££ Old Hall House, Heart of England Conference & Events Centre, Meriden Rd, Fillongley, CV7 8DX, T01676-540333, www.heartofengland.co.uk. A welcoming B&B on the large grounds of a conference centre.

❼ Restaurants

Stratford-upon-Avon p33, map p34
Stratford restaurants are an amiable mix of beautiful country pubs – some of which have had the 'gastro' makeover – and smart, if a little old-school, silver service-type establishments. And, of course, this being the Midlands, there are plenty of curry houses to choose from.

££ Bamboodle, Union St, T01789-414999. Serving Asian-style street food in modern, upmarket surroundings; live music on Fri.

££ El Greco, Rother St, T01789-290505. Excellent Greek food in this contemporary restaurant overlooking the market square.

££ Essence, Old Red Lion Court, Bridge St, T01789-269999. Modern British, both in terms of the food and the decor. Good quality ingredients and an excellent wine list to accompany them.

££ Lamb's Restaurant, Sheep St, T01789-292554. Stylish and modern, this popular restaurant still retains a cosy feel in one of the oldest buildings in Stratford.

££ Marlowe's Restaurant, 1st floor, 18 High St, T01789-204999. A stunning, late 16th-century building with an Elizabethan dining room, though it is rather formal and prides itself on its silver service.

££ The Opposition Bistro, Sheep St, T01789-269980. Modern, bustling bistro in a historical building.

££ Sorrento, 8 Ely St, T01789-297999. Italian trattoria, simply but elegantly decorated with a pleasant easy-going atmosphere.

££ Thespians, 26 Sheep St, T01789-267187, www.thespiansltd.com. There's an army of smiling, extremely courteous staff in this place which, despite its name, specializes in north Indian and Bangladeshi cuisine.

£ Aladdin's, Tiddington Main St, Tiddington Rd, T01789-294491. Friendly curry house, reasonably priced, recommended by locals.

Cafés

Box Brownie Coffee, Henley St. Nice little café that does great coffee.

Leamington Spa *p36*

£££-££ Emperor's, Bath Pl, CV31 3BP, T1926-313030, www.emperorsrestaurant. co.uk. Excellent Chinese restaurant serving Cantonese fare. You need to book in advance to eat here.

£££-££ Oscar's, Chandos St, CV32 4RL, T01926-452807, www.oscarsfrenchbistro. co.uk. A small French bistro that's probably not for you if you like lots of space. The good menu changes regularly, and there's a decent wine list.

££ Le Bistrot Pierre, 28 Park St, CV32 4QN, T01926-426261, www.lebistrotpierre.co.uk. Popular French chain restaurant offering pre-theatre specials and dishes such as steak and quiche. Some offerings not as Gallic as you'd expect.

££ Momenti, 9 Regent Place, CV31 1EH, T01926-888895. This friendly Italian place serves tasty dishes made from fresh ingredients, and the meat options are particularly good.

££-£ The Basement Restaurant, 1 Spencer St, CV31 3NE, T01926-887288, www. basementrestaurant.com. A budget option with quite a lot going for it, not least the live music it hosts on a regular basis.

££-£ Kayal, 42 Regent St, CV32 5EG, T01926-314800, www.kayalrestaurant. com. South Indian cuisine in modern surroundings, try the biryani.

££-£ Paprika Club, 22 Regent St, CV32 5EH, T01926-428272, www.paprikaclub.co.uk. An original take on the traditional curry house with cool decor and good food simply prepared and reasonably priced.

££-£ Wagamama, Old Regent Hotel, 95 Parade Royal, CV32 4AY, T01926-833245, www.wagamama.com. Usual Wagamama fare but this restaurant is worth visiting to enjoy the building of the **Old Regent Hotel** with its high ceilings. The atmosphere gives the chain restaurant a little something extra.

Warwick *p36*

£££-££ Tailors, 22 Market Place, CV34 4SL, T01926-410590, www.tailorsrestaurant.com. One of the best restaurants in Warwick and fine dining, so make sure you book in advance to secure a table. Dishes are innovative and there are a range of menus, including the taster menu one dedicated to vegetarians.

££ ASK, 16/18 High St, CV34 4AP, T01926-409809, www.askitalian.co.uk. A chain restaurant serving Italian staples such as pizza and pasta. A good lunch option.

££ Giovanni's Restaurant, 15 Smith St, Warwick, CV34 4JA, T01926-494904. A friendly and unsurprising Italian restaurant, though try to avoid the large parties of office workers out for an upmarket works do.

££ Pancho Tapas Bar, 5-6 The Knibbs, Smith St, CV34 4UW, T01926-400809, www.iampancho.co.uk. Once the Cellar

Restaurant, this is now a popular tapas place with a good atmosphere.

£ Thomas Oken Tea Rooms, 20 Castle St, CV34 4BP, T1926-499307, www.thomasoken tearooms.com. What a tea room should be, with loose leafed teas, delicious tea cakes and afternoon tea, and savoury options such as sandwiches, soups and cooked breakfast. Recommended.

Coventry *p39*

££ Browns, Earl St, T0247-622 1100, www. brownsindependentbar.com. This isn't part of the Brown's chain. This restaurant serves freshly prepared dishes, and has a strong veggie menu, a pleasant ambience and a terrace overlooking the Cathedral.

££ Court 6, 16 Spon St, T0247-655 9190. Offers excellent Indian/Pakistani dishes in friendly and comfortable surrounds.

££ Millsy's Café and Bar and the **Gallery Restaurant**, 20 Earlsden St, Earlsden, CV5 6EG, T0247-671 3222, www.millsys.co.uk. 2 decent dining experiences in one location serving contemporary cuisine. **Millsy's** also hosts regular live music.

££ Ristorante Etna, 54 Hertford Pl, CV1 1LB, T0247-622 3183, www.etnarestaurant. co.uk. An old-school Italian trattoria, much patronized by the locals, with Sicilian cuisine as well as the usual Italian fare.

££ Thai Dusit, London Rd, CV1 2JP, T0247-622 7788, www.coventry.thaidusit.co.uk. A good Thai restaurant with the spiciness of the food clearly marked.

££-£ Cheylsmore Balti, 171 Daventry Rd, CV3 5HF, T0247-650 6147. A reasonable balti house, though don't expect Brummie standards. It is open late on Fri and Sat.

££-£ The Dragon Phoenix, Hertford Pl, The Butts, CV1 3JZ, T0247-625 8688, www.dragon-phoenix.co.uk. Italian, Indian and Chinese buffet. Popular with groups, and the place to come if you're hungry.

Stratford-upon-Avon *p33, map p34*
The College Arms, Lower Quinton, T01789-720342. An historic 16th-century inn on the edge of the Cotswolds, originally owned by Henry VIII.

Dirty Duck, Waterside, T01789-297312. The ultimate luvvies pub in Stratford, frequented by members of the RSC and the multitude of hangers-on that the theatre world has always attracted.

The Encore, Bridge St, T01789-269462. Stylish gastropub near the river.

Garrick Inn, High St, T01789-292186. This is the place to come if you like your pubs seriously beautiful and like a movie set from Olde Englande. The beer's not bad, either.

The Lamplighter, Rother St, T01789-293071. Traditional local pub, with beer garden, opposite the Civic Hall.

The Old Thatch Tavern, Greenhill St, T01789-295216. Small, homely little pub that has been a licensed premises since 1623. Nice little courtyard garden, very popular for food.

Othello's, Chapel St, T01789-269427. Upmarket bar and brasserie attached to the Mercure Shakespeare.

Pen and Parchment, Bridgefoot, T01789-297697. A traditional pub with a contemporary twist, and a large beer garden.

The Vintner, 4-5 Sheep St, T01789-297259. A wine bar – as you might expect – and restaurant, named for the vintner who lived in this building in 1600.

The Windmill Inn, Church St, T01789-297687. Friendly Greene King pub with a network of cosy, really picturesque rooms that are begging to be occupied for at least an entire day of supping cask ales.

Coventry *p39*
The town has always loved partying, so you'd expect to find lots of drinking holes, plus of course some nightclubs of a rather dubious stripe.

The Beer Engine, Far Gosford St, CV1 5DW. Once known for its real ale and live music –

before being turned into a student bikini bar – **The Beer Engine** locals loved is back. New landlords and a refurb have resulted in a cosy interior and local talent performing at weekends.

The Golden Cross, 8 Hay La, CV1 5RF, T0247-622 2311. This place claims to have been a student pub since 1583. It's really a classic city centre boozer built on the site of a medieval mint. The place to come for live music at weekends.

The Old Windmill, 22 Spon St, CV1 3BA, T0247-625 2183, www.old-windmill-inn.co.uk. Another great reason for visiting this historic street, this is the oldest and possibly the nicest pub in the city. It sells great real ale and some interesting English wines such as elderberry, sloe and mead. Beautiful beams, real fires and a warren of pannelled rooms.

🎵 Entertainment

Stratford-upon-Avon *p33, map p34*
Music
The Bandstand on the Recreation Ground has bands on some Sun afternoons during the summer.
Civic Hall, 14 Rother St, box office T01789-414513, www.civichall.co.uk. The venue for variety shows, classical music, big band, pantomime and dance nights. Licensed bar.

Theatre
Royal Shakespeare Company, www.rsc.org.uk, ticket hotline T0844-8001110, Mon-Sat 1000-1800, £14-60, discounts available.

🎪 Festivals

Stratford-upon-Avon *p33, map p34*
Apr Shakespeare's Birthday Celebrations. Morris dancing, street entertainers, the ceremony of the unfurling of the flags, the floral procession of dignitaries from all over the world between the Birthplace and Holy Trinity Church, dancing by local children and much more.

May Stratford-upon-Avon English Music Festival, held biennially, an extravaganza of all kinds of music.
Jun Stratford Regatta, on the River Avon.
Jul Stratford-upon-Avon International Flute Festival, free, lasts for about a fortnight.
Oct Stratford Mop Fair. The central streets of Stratford are closed to traffic for this annual traditional street fair with fairground rides, stalls, and the roasting of a whole ox, the first piece of which is auctioned for charity by the Mayor. It is one of the biggest mop fairs in the country.

🛍 Shopping

Stratford-upon-Avon *p33, map p34*
Antiques
The Barn Antiques Centre 5 miles from Stratford, T01789-721399. The largest antique centre in south Warwickshire, it's crammed full of collectables, bygones and antiques.

Clothes
Stratford-upon-Avon has a surprisingly decent collection of clothes shops. You'll find many of the usual high-street fashion staples on Bridge, Shrieve and Wood streets. If you're in need of 'fashion therapy', try **Gemini** at 15 Wood St, or **Gemini Shoes**, 3 Cook's Alley, where the proprietor offers healing hands for the fashion traumatized. **Littlejohn**, on Wood St, is a retailer that stocks only items designed in the UK, or supplied by UK companies. For something a bit different, try **Humbug Vintage** on Shreive Walk, which is home to hand-picked vintage items from around the world, but is still pretty affordable. For trinkets or foodie gifts, look for **Vinegar Hill** on Meer St; **Vin Neuf** on Union St; **Benson's House of Tea** on Henley St, or the **The Stratford Sweet Shop**, Henley St.

Markets
Selling of a more basic kind happens at the famous traditional Chartered Markets (all over town, but particularly on Market Sq),

which still take place every week throughout the year. Stratford has been a market place for centuries, receiving its charters over 800 years ago. **The Farmer's Market** takes place twice monthly on Market Sq, just off Rother St, where you can buy superb fresh produce from some of the best farming land in the country.

What to do

Stratford-upon-Avon *p33, map p34*
Air
Wickers World Balloon Flights,
launch from the Stratford-upon-Avon race course, Luddington Rd, T01889-882222, www.wickersworld.co.uk.

Boating
Avon Boating, The Boathouse, Swan's Nest Ln, T01789-267073. Hire small boats or take a passenger cruise from this 100-year old boathouse.
Bancroft Cruisers,, Bridgefoot, T01789-269669, for guided sightseeing cruises.

Golf
Ingon Manor Golf & Country Club, Ingon Ln, T01789-731857.
Stratford Golf Club, Tiddington Rd, T01789-205749.
Stratford Oaks, Bearley Rd, Snitterfield, T01789-731980.

Gliding
Bidford Gliding Centre, Honeybourne Rd, Bidford-on-Avon, T01789-778807.
Stratford-upon-Avon Gliding Club, Snitterfield Airfield, Snitterfield Rd, Bearley, T01789-731095.

Horse racing
Stratford-upon-Avon Racecourse, Luddington Rd, T01789-267949.

Horse riding
WJ Pettigrew, Ettington Park Stables, T01789-450653.

The Sport Horse Training Centre, The Wolds, The Green, Snitterfield, T01789-730222.

Tennis
Stratford Lawn Tennis Club, Swan's Nest Ln, T01789-295801.

Transport

Stratford-upon-Avon *p33, map p34*
Bicycle
Stratford Bike Hire, Stratford Greenway, Seven Meadows Rd, T07711-776340, closed in winter.

Bus
National Express, T08717-818178, run 3 direct services per day from **London Victoria** and one from **Birmingham** (1 hr).

Car
Enterprise Rent-A-Car, Unit 8, Swan Trade Centre, T01789-403920; **Hertz Rent-a-car**, Station Rd, T01789-298827.

Taxi
Ranks are situated in Wood St, Rother St and Bridge St, at Bridgefoot and at the railway station. **Shakespeare Taxis**, 17 Greenhill St, T01789-266100; 24/7 Taxis, Shottery, T01789-415668.

Train
Stratford Station is off the Alcester Rd. For timetable details check www.stratfordstation.com. There are **Chiltern Railways** services to **London** every 2 hrs, and **London Midland** trains to **Birmingham** are hourly.

Leamington Spa *p36*
Bus
Leamington is well served by bus and coach with frequent **National Express**, www.nationalexpress.com, services from the north and south.

Car

Leamington is within easy striking distance of the extensive motorway network in the area. From north and south via the M40 take junctions 14 and 15, or the M1. Travelling from the west-south-west, take the M5 and leave it at Bromsgrove picking up the M42.

Taxi

A2B Taxis, 15 Cranmer Grove, CV34 6EP, T01926-470048, www.a2b-taxis.co.uk, chauffeured cars; **Avon Knight Cars**, 15 High St, CV31 3AW, T01926-420041; **Dialacab**, 13 Maple Rd, CV31 3HA, T01926-882965.

Train

Chiltern Railways, www.chilternrailways.co.uk, run 2 trains an hour from **London Marylebone** (1 hr 30 mins). There are also trains from **Paddington**. Coming from the north there are services from either **Birmingham Snow Hill** or less frequent but quicker services from **New Street**. From the East and West Midlands and from East Anglia, Manchester and Wales, **Crosscountry**, www.crosscountry trains.co.uk, run frequent services.

❶ Directory

Stratford-upon-Avon *p33, map p34*
Hospitals Stratford Hospital, Arden St, T01789-205831. Minor injuries unit daily 0900-1700. **Warwick Hospital**, Lakin Rd, Warwick, T01926-495321. 24 hr A&E. **Arden Medical Centre**, Albany Rd, T01789-414942. Post office: Henley St, T01789-268869.
Library Public library on Henley St, T0300-555 8171. See page 35 for details of Shakespeare Centre Library.
Police Rother St, T01789-414111.

Coventry *p39*
Hospitals Coventry and Warwickshire University Hospital, Clifford Bridge Rd, CV2 2DX, T0247-6964000. **Police** Little Park Police Station, Little Park Rd, CV1 2JX, T0845-113 5000.

Northamptonshire and Bedfordshire

Both these Midland counties are usually overlooked by visitors, not without some reason, although Northamptonshire embraces some beautiful countryside dotted with old stone-built villages, grand stately homes and innumerable church spires. Bedfordshire's defining character derives from the broad floodplain of the River Ouse, its clay soil traditionally used for bricks. The greensand ridge in the middle of the county is its most attractive feature but there is also the much-publicized safari park and stately home at Woburn Abbey at its western end, and quaint Victorian estate villages such as Old Warden at its eastern. Folded combes and windswept downs fan out from Barton. Bedford itself is chiefly famous for bricks, hats and being the place of imprisonment of John Bunyan. Northamptonshire boasts some very grand houses indeed, most impressively the Duke of Buccleuch's pad at Boughton and most popularly Althorp, last resting place of Diana, Princess of Wales.

Northampton and around → *For listings, see pages 54-55.*

The county of 'squires, spires and mires' attracts fewer visitors than it deserves, perhaps because it's generally perceived to be in the middle of nowhere. The M1 slices through the southeastern part on its way north. Northampton itself sits right beside the motorway, ruined by recent developments but concealing some extraordinary churches and an unusual collection of footwear. Shoemaking once made this part of the country famous, although its wealth has always come from manufacturing industry and agriculture, both currently down on their luck. Large estates cover most of its northern part, the most spectacular and pompous being Boughton House, the most popular, for mawkish reasons, being Althorp. Otherwise the pleasures of the county are to be found in exploring its small villages, especially along the valley of the River Nene, with its fine gardens and churches.

Arriving in Northampton

Getting there Northampton is on the main London–Birmingham line, with regular services running into London Euston (one hour). Northampton is just off the M1, easily reached in one hour 30 minutes from London. **National Express** ① *www.nationalexpress. com*, run direct coaches to Northampton every three hours or so, taking just over two hours from London Victoria.

Getting around Town buses are run by **First Northampton** ① *www.firstgroup.com*, and the network of local buses to outlying villages by **Stagecoach** ① *www.stagecoachbus.com*. Northampton itself can easily be walked around, but exploring beyond the town really requires a car.

Information **Northampton TIC** ① *Royal and Derngate Theatres, NN1 1DP, T01604-838800, Mon-Sat 1000-1700, Sun 1400-1700.* **Oundle TIC** ① *14 West St, PE8 4EF, T01832-274333, Mon-Sat 0900-1700.*

Northampton

Northampton was once synonymous with shoemaking. As recently as the 1930s, almost half the town's population were cobblers of one sort or another. Today it's a fairly unprepossessing modern market town with little to suggest its ancient roots except a handful of fine churches. Charles II destroyed the Norman castle on his restoration but the **Church of the Holy Sepulchre** survives, one of the four round churches still standing in England. Like the castle, it was built by the Norman knight Simon de Senlis, inspired by his crusading experiences and looking more like the one in Jerusalem than the others. Its heavy rounded columns in a ring are original, topped with late 14th-century arches.

A few steps southeast from the church down Sheep Street is the wide expanse of **Market Square**, the centre of modern Northampton and still used for a market of sorts most days of the week. Just to the south again, **All Saints Church** is a wonderful late-17th-century building, a vivid essay in Baroque enlivening the town centre. Its echoing interior is covered with a dome, a kind of mini-St Pauls. The poet John Clare used to worship here.

Further south, towards the train station, St Giles Square contains the Victorian neo-Gothic **Guildhall** and opposite, the local **Northampton Museum and Art Gallery** ① *Guildhall Rd, NN1 1DP, T01604-838111, www.northampton.gov.uk/museums, Tue-Sat 1000-1700, Sun 1400-1700, free,* contains an extensive boot and shoe collection. The Followers of Fashion Gallery displays Manolo Blaniks down the ages, as it were, while the

Life and Sole Gallery charts the history of the shoe. The most popular exhibits are the DMs worn in 'Tommy', and a shoe made for an elephant.

Around Northampton

Five miles northwest of Northampton is one of the county's most popular visitor attractions, for the saddest of reasons. **Althorp** ① *NN7 4HQ, off A428 to Rugby, T01604-770107, www.spencerofalthorp.com, Jul-Aug grounds and exhibition 1200-1700, house 1300-1700 (last admission 1600), see website for prices, cheaper if pre-booked*, has been the stately seat of the Spencer family for the last few hundred years but is now much more famous for being the childhood home and last resting place of Diana, Princess of Wales. Her grave lies on an island in the middle of a lake overlooked by a classical temple restored in her memory. As well as an exhibition of some of her personal effects, the house also contains an internationally renowned collection of paintings by Gainsborough, Reynolds, Van Dyck and others.

More elegant gardens can be seen six miles north at **Cottesbrooke Hall** ① *NN6 8PF, T01604-505808, www.cottesbrooke.co.uk, May-Jun Wed-Thu 1400-1730, Jul, Aug and Sep Thu 1400-1730, house and gardens £8, child £4, gardens only £5.50, child £3*. Very refined, they were designed around an almost unaltered Queen Anne mansion, supposedly the model for Jane Austen's *Mansfield Park* and laid out by a variety of eminent designers in the last century. They include a philosophers' walk, Dutch garden, water gardens and a formal garden.

Near the village of Rushton, nine miles to the northeast, five miles northwest of Kettering, a **Triangular Lodge** ① *(EH), NN14 1RP, T01536-710761, see website for opening hours, £3.30, concessions £3, child £2*, was built by Sir Thomas Tresham in 1597 for his rabbit-breeder. A devout Catholic, Sir Thomas designed a tricksome fantasy of a place in honour of the Holy Trinity. The three-sided building stands in the park of Rushton Hall and is embellished with all kinds of arcane religious symbolism. It's now the highlight of a 'Tresham Trail' round the area.

Four miles northeast of Kettering stands the palatial Northamptonshire home of the Duke of Buccleuch, **Boughton House** ① *NN14 1BJ, T01536-515731, www.boughtonhouse.org.uk, house and gardens open daily throughout Aug, house 1400-1700 (last entry 1600), gardens 1200-1700, £10, child £7, gardens only £5, child £2*, which has been compared to Versailles. The grounds include acres of parkland, lakes and long tree-lined avenues. The house itself took on its current imposing French appearance in the late 17th century and contains an array of Old Masters and fine furniture.

East of Boughton toward Thrapston the landscape opens up into the valley of the River Nene. **Oundle** is a quiet little town dominated by an exclusive private school. A few miles downstream, the riverside village of **Wadenhoe** is often cited as the most picturesque in the county. Just to the north, **Fotheringhay** has a remarkable church, the first thing that strikes visitors, whether arriving by road or river. The tower was designed for a much larger church that no longer exists. The castle that once stood on the mound nearby was thoroughly dismantled by James I for the role it had played in the death of his mother, Mary Queen of Scots, in 1587. Her traumatic execution involved several blows of the axe, the interference of the Queen's dog and a loose wig.

East of Northampton, it's worth seeking out the stately splendours of the Marquess of Northampton's home at **Castle Ashby** ① *NN7 1LQ, T01604-695200, www.castleashbygardens.co.uk, see website for opening hours, £5, child £4.50*. The grounds include an Italian garden, an orangery and lakeside walks.

Just to the north across the valley of the Nene, Earls Barton has a famous Saxon tower. In **Jeyes of Earls Barton** ① *26 The Square, NN6 0AN, T01604-810289, www.jeyesofearlsbarton. co.uk*, you'll find the Earls Barton Museum of Village Life, with an exhibition of Earls Barton footwear manufacture, a collection of early photographs and other local memorabilia.

Seven miles south of Northampton, **Stoke Bruerne** is England's most famous canal village, approached by a flight of seven locks from the River Tove. The canal forms the main road, and there's a museum of barge life. Just up the way is the **Blisworth Tunnel**. Boats can be hired from **Blisworth Tunnel Narrowboats** ① *Mill Wharf, Gayton Rd, Blisworth, NN7 3BN, T01604-858868, www.millwharfboats.co.uk*, to explore the 3000-yard long Blisworth Tunnel. It has no towpath so all boats once had to be 'legged' through the watery darkness.

Bedfordshire → *For listings, see pages 54-55.*

Anyone interested in the history of the Christian church or dissenters in general will want to look in on the John Bunyan museum in Bedford itself, as well as the Moot Hall at Elstow just outside. Fans of Glen Miller and Second World War airfields will be pleased to discover the exhibition in the musician's honour at Twinwood. On a similar theme, the Shuttleworth Collection in Old Warden has seven hangars-worth of historical aviation exhibits. Otherwise, the county's top visitor attraction is Woburn Abbey and Safari Park, a less colourful but just as well publicized version of Longleat in Wiltshire.

Arriving in Bedfordshire

Getting there Bedford is connected via **First Capital Connect** to London St Pancras (just over an hour). East Midlands trains go from St Pancras to Bedford (40 minutes) and then on to Leicester (one hour from Bedford), Nottingham (one hour 30 minutes from Bedford) and Sheffield (one hour 40 minutes from Bedford). Bedford can be reached easily from London on either the A1 or M1 in around an hour. **National Express** ① *www.nationalexpress.com*, run regularly from London Victoria to Bedford.

Information Bedford TIC ① *10 St Paul's Sq, MK40 1SJ, T01234-718112, www.visitbedford. co.uk, daily Mon-Sat 09-1630*. **Mid-Bedfordshire TIC** ① *5 Shannon Ct, High St, Sandy, SG19 1AG, T01767-682728. Apr-Oct Mon-Sat 1000-1630, Sat, Sun 1000-1500, Nov-Mar Mon-Fri 1000-1600, Sat 1000-1500.*

Bedford

The county town of Bedford, famous for once making quantities of bricks and hats, is now a pleasant enough large town on the banks of the river Great Ouse. The river is crossed at the southern end of the High Street, from where the Embankment runs along the waterside. Not much remains of the Norman castle except a mound in the park near Castle Lane. Formerly known as the Higgins Art Gallery & Museum, **The Higgins** ① *T01234-718618, www.cecilhigginsartgallery.org*, has undergone extensive refurbishment and is due to open in mid 2013. Local history displays and an exceptional collection of watercolours, sculpture, furniture, glass, ceramics and metalwork will be exhibited. The watercolour collection includes works by the likes of Turner, Constable, Blake, Landseer, Sickert, Lowry, Hepworth, Nicholson and Henry Moore among others.

In Mill Street, the bronze doors of the **Bunyan Meeting Free Church** were donated by the Duke of Bedford in 1876, with 10 panels depicting scenes from *The Pilgrim's Progress*. Written by the preacher and Parliamentarian John Bunyan while he was imprisoned in

Bedford jail for 12 years under Charles II's religious laws, it still ranks as one of the most influential pieces of Christian literature of all time. Bunyan bought a barn and orchard on his release from prison, which in 1707 was replaced by a Meeting House, and in 1850 by the church that stands here today. Next door, the **John Bunyan Museum** ⓘ *Bunyan Meeting, Mill St, MK40 3EU, T01234-213722, www.bunyanmeeting.co.uk, Feb-Nov Tue-Sat 1100-1600*, was opened in 1998, displaying exhibits and artefacts associated with his life and an illustrated display on *The Pilgrim's Progress*.

Around Bedfordshire

The late-15th-century **Moot Hall** ⓘ *Easter-Sep Sat 1300-1600*, at Elstow, was where John Bunyan saw the light while mucking about on the green opposite (he was born here in 1628). Moot Hall is now a museum of 17th-century English life and tradition.

Fans of Second World War big band music will want to take a trip to the **Glen Miller Museum** ⓘ *Twinwood Airfield, T01234-350413, www.twinwoodairfield.co.uk, May-Oct Sun 1030-1600, £4*, where there are also a number of other small museums. There's another museum at Thurleigh, the **306 Bombardment Group Museum** ⓘ *T01234-708715, www.306bg.co.uk, Mar-Oct Sat-Sun 1030-1600, £3*. On the 9 October 1942 a formation of B17 Flying Fortress left Thurleigh on the first of what was to be 341 daylight bombing missions over occupied Europe. Thurleigh airfield became the first base in England to be handed over completely to the Americans, giving them full sovereignty and control of these few acres. The museum is housed in the original airfield's control tower.

Set in a 3000-acre deer park, **Woburn Abbey** ⓘ *Woburn Park, MK17 9WA, T01525-290333, www.woburn.co.uk/abbey, see website for opening times. Take exit 13 off the M1 motorway, or leave the A5 at Hockliffe for the A4012, the Abbey is well signed from here*, is the home of the Marquess and Marchioness of Tavistock and their family, and houses one of the most important private art collections in the world, including paintings by Van Dyck, Gainsborough, Reynolds, and Canaletto as well as 18th-century French and English furniture, silver, gold and porcelain. Visitors can also enjoy the renowned antiques centre, coffee shop, gift shops, pottery and beautiful grounds including a safari park.

Opened in 1931 as the first open zoo in Europe, **Whipsnade** ⓘ *Dunstable, LU6 2LF, the zoo is signposted from the M1 (junctions 9 and 12) and all major roads, T0844-225 1826, www.zsl.org/zsl-whipsnade-zoo/, Mar-Sep 1000-1800, Oct-Feb 1000-1600, £21, child £16*, is now the largest zoo in the UK and the country base of London Zoo. Larger animals, such as elephants, have been gradually moved here from the city.

The **Shuttleworth Collection** ⓘ *Shuttleworth (Old Warden) Aerodrome, Nr Biggleswade, SG18 9EP, T01767-627927, www.shuttleworth.org, Apr-Oct daily 0930-1700, Nov-Mar daily 0930-1600, £12, under-16s free*, off the A1, near Sandy, about 12 miles east of Bedford, is an impressive museum of antique aircraft, biplanes and triplanes, as well as the Swiss Gardens (closed until early 2015), and a bird of prey centre in Old Warden Park. **Cockayne Hatley**, 10 miles east of Bedford on the border with Cambridgeshire, has one of the most remarkable parish church interiors in the country in its church of St John. Furnished with loot from the Napoleonic Wars by Henry Cockayne Cust including the choir from the Abbey of Oignies, the poet WE Henley, friend of both Robert Louis Stevenson and JM Barrie, and his daughter, who is said to have been the model for Wendy in 'Peter Pan', are buried in the churchyard.

For hotel and restaurant price codes and other relevant information, see pages 9-12.

🛏 Where to stay

Northampton and around *p50*

££ Coach House Hotel, 8-10 East Park Pde, Kettering Rd, Northampton, NN1 4LE, T01604-757448, www.thecoachhouse northampton.co.uk. 10 mins east of the centre, has seen better days but friendly.

££ Poplars Hotel, Cross St, Moulton, NN3 7RZ, T1604 643 983, www.thepoplars hotel.com. A lovely little hotel with rooms in the main house or courtyard annexe.

££-£ The Legacy Lime Trees Hotel, 7-9 Langham Pl, Barrack Rd, Northampton, NN2 6AA, T08444-119480, www.legacy-hotels.co.uk. Half a mile north of the centre, reasonable enough hotel, favourably priced.

£ The Elms, Kislingbury, near Northampton (4 miles west), NN7 4AH, T01604-830326. Comfortable rooms on a working farm.

£ The King's Head, Church St, Wadenhoe, near Oundle, PE8 5ST, T01832-720024, www.wadenhoekingshead.co.uk. In a conservation village, the *King's Head* on the River Nene is a popular focal point for the area, with a variety of different bars, good food and a couple of bedrooms.

£ Wold Farm, Harrington Rd, Old, near Northampton (8 miles north), NN6 9RJ, T01604-781258, www.woldfarm.co.uk. Charming 18th-century house with glorious gardens, a billiard table, and good breakfasts.

Bedford and around *p52*

££££-£££ Swan Hotel, The Embankment, MK40 1RW, T01234-346565, www.bedford swanhotel.co.uk. This elegant spa hotel is in the heart of Bedford, built in 1794 for the Duke of Bedford. The staircase now in use here originally came from Houghton House in Ampthill, reputedly the inspiration for 'House Beautiful' in *The Pilgrim's Progress*.

£££ The Embankment Hotel, The Embankment, MK40 3PD, T01234-261332. Impressive black and white building overlooking the River Great Ouse.

££ Bedford Park House, 59 De Pary's Av, MK40 2TR, T01234-215100. Lovely Victorian House in tree-lined avenue, close to town centre.

£ Tithe Farm, Renhold, MK41 OLX, T01234-771364. Farmhouse (16th-century) with secure parking, 5 miles from Bedford.

£ Travel Lodge, Brickhill Dr, Saturn Heights, MK41 7PH, T0871-984 6276, www.travelodge.co.uk. Not the greatest of surroundings and a couple of miles from town, but rooms are clean and good value.

🍴 Restaurants

Northampton and around *p50*

£££-££ The Falcon Inn, Fotheringay, PE8 5HZ, T01832-226254, www.thefalcon-inn.co.uk. Top quality food served up in this polite village local.

££ The Shuckburgh Arms, Stoke Doyle, near Oundle, PE8 5TG, T01832-272339, www.shuckburgh-arms.co.uk. A cosy stone-built pub a couple of miles west of Oundle with a log fire and rooms.

££-£ The Dining Room, 82 Derngate, NN1 1UH, T01604-230166, www.thediningroom.org. The real reason to come here is for afternoon tea – savoury for starters, sweet for afters – and they're so busy it's best to book in advance to secure a table. The homemade cakes are delicious. There are also tasty lunch specials. Recommended.

Bedford and around *p52*

££ Bengal Brasserie 9 The Broadway, MK40 2TJ, T01234-341444, www.bengal brasseriebedford.co.uk. Busy restaurant, offering Bangladeshi and Indian cuisine.

££ Carpenter's Arms, 1 Horton Rd, Slapton, near Leighton Buzzard, LU7 9DB, T01525-

220563, www.carpentersarmsslapton.co.uk. Rambling old 16th-century village pub with an above-average menu, well-kept real ales and a long stone's throw from the Grand Union Canal.

££-£ Pizzeria Santaniello, 9-11 Newnham St, MK40 3JR, T01234-353742, www.pizzeria santaniello.com. Original family-run pizza and pasta restaurant. Traditional family fare and atmosphere.

£ Polhill Arms, 25 Wilden Rd, Renhold, MK41 0JP, T01234-771398, www.polhillarms. co.uk. Welcoming pub with open fire, good ales and tasty pub grub.

Oxfordshire

Very much the capital of its county, England's oldest and most famous university town (once dubbed 'the home of lost causes' by the poet Matthew Arnold) rarely disappoints. Arnold noted that, when seen from a distance, the city's spires, turrets and domes seem to be dreaming. Walking around the old stone colleges or through their surrounding meadows and gardens, it's impossible not to be aware of the weight of centuries of scholarship, culture and learning. Thankfully, though, the streets are as alive today as they've ever been. More urban and spacious than Cambridge, its equally celebrated sister in the east, Oxford continues to be one of the most remarkable, least isolated and most intellectually engaging of modern European cities.

To the west, the Thames comes wandering in over a wide and fertile plain, past Kelmscott, Buscot and medieval manor houses such as Stanton Harcourt. To the northwest, the Windrush Valley is dotted with exceptionally attractive stone villages such as Minster Lovell, between the old market town of Witney and the honey-stone bustle of Burford, where the Cotswolds begin.

Issues Summary

18/09/2017 12:29

Comhairle Chontae Átha Cliath Theas
South Dublin County Libraries - Ballyroan

Id :: ************92

Item SD900000104815, Heart of England
09-10-17

Total Number of Issued Items **1**

Oxford *→ For listings, see pages 69-74.*

Oxford's name means many things to most people: above all though, it's still a university city of international standing. First-time visitors can hardly fail to be impressed by the sheer number of beautiful old colleges that make up this pinnacle of British academe. And it comes as some surprise that in the 21st century these mellow stone buildings, with their beamed halls, chapels, quads and spires, continue to be used pretty much for their original purpose. Christ Church is the grandest, Merton the oldest, New College the most authentic in its groundplan and Magdalen the loveliest, but all the colleges in the centre of the city are worth looking around. Unfortunately, they have an ambivalent attitude to opening their doors to casual observers, making access unpredictable (although most are open at some time in the afternoon). The colleges aside, there's so much else in the city to enjoy, not least two of the most extraordinary museums in the country: the Ashmolean and the Pitt Rivers. Views over the 'dreaming spires' can be had from several church towers in the middle of town. The Botanical Gardens are a delightful retreat on the riverside, next to flowering water meadows just beyond the old city walls. And then there's punting on the river, almost a mandatory activity in summer for students and visitors alike. If all the boats are booked up, simply taking a stroll in the green acres so close to the city centre makes for an exceedingly pleasant afternoon. As one of Europe's most remarkable cities, Oxford is, of course, mobbed in high season. That said, it's never too difficult to escape the crowds, and even the passing visitor is likely to appreciate the highly charged meeting of cerebral old institutions with bright young things.

Arriving in Oxford

Getting there Trains from London Paddington run very regularly and take between one and two hours; those via Reading usually have fewer stops than those going via Didcot Parkway. Oxford's one-way road system has reduced motorists to tears, and parking is almost impossible in the middle of the city without paying through the nose. However, there are several **Park & Ride** options. Thornhill Park and Ride, to the west, and Seacourt, to the east, are served by bus number 400 and tend to fill up very early in the day; bus 300 serves Pear Tree Park and Ride (to the north) and Redbridge (to the south). Water Eaton Park & Ride, a little further north, takes you into town by bus 500, and despite being further out, is often one of the quickest routes into the centre. If you must arrive on four wheels, you'll find Oxford just off the M40, about an hour from London, half an hour from the M25. Oxford is very well served by **coach** companies. ►► *For further details, see Transport, page 74.*

Getting around **Walking** or **cycling** around central Oxford is one of life's real pleasures. For some of the slightly further-flung parts of the city, **taxis** are relatively cheap and the **bus** network from Gloucester Green along the High Street and around Carfax is regular and reliable. The centre of the city of Oxford is Carfax, the crossroads at the top of the High Street. Pedestrianized Cornmarket heads north from Carfax into wide St Giles, eventually leading to Woodstock and Banbury. High Street stretches east to Magdalen Bridge, while Queen Street continues west, down past the Norman Castle and prison towards the train station. St Aldate's slopes downhill south, past Christ Church College, with its prominent Tom Tower, crossing the Thames at Folly Bridge and continuing out of town as the Abingdon Road.

Oxford

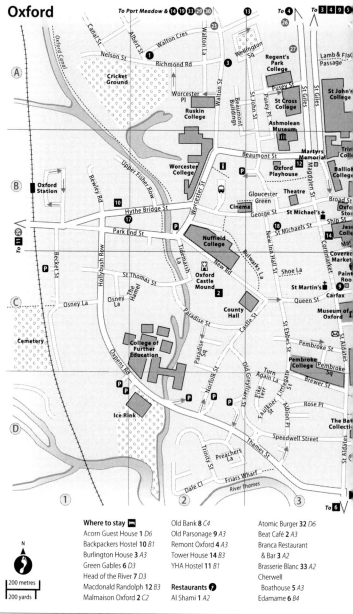

Where to stay 🛏
Acorn Guest House **1** D6
Backpackers Hostel **10** B1
Burlington House **3** A3
Green Gables **6** D3
Head of the River **7** D3
Macdonald Randolph **12** B3
Malmaison Oxford **2** C2

Old Bank **8** C4
Old Parsonage **9** A3
Remont Oxford **4** A3
Tower House **14** B3
YHA Hostel **11** B1

Restaurants 🍴
Al Shami **1** A2

Atomic Burger **32** D6
Beat Café **2** A3
Branca Restaurant
  & Bar **3** A2
Brasserie Blanc **33** A2
Cherwell
  Boathouse **5** A3
Edamame **6** B4

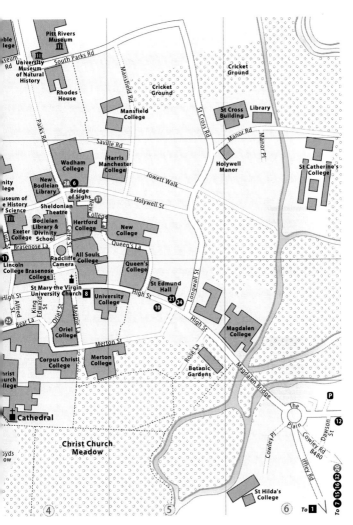

Gardeners Arms **4** A3
Gee's **8** A3
Golden Cross Pizza
  Express **9** C3
Grand Café **10** C5
Jericho Café **14** A2
Kazbar **15** D6
Malikas **7** D6

Missing Bean **11** B4
Moya **12** D6
Peppers Burgers **19** A2
Pierre Victoire Bistrot **13** A3
Quarter Horse Coffee **16** D6
Queen's Lane
  Coffee House **21** C5
Rose **24** C5

SoJo **17** B1
Zappi's Bike Café **18** B3

Pubs & bars 🍺
Bear **25** C4
Café Tarifa **20** D6
Duke of Cambridge **26** A3
Eagle & Child **27** A3

The House **22** C4
King's Arms **28** B4
Perch **29** B1 or A2
Raoul's Bar **23** A3
Trout Inn **30** A2
Turf Tavern **31** B4

Information The **TIC** ① *15-16 Broad St, T01865-252200, www.visitoxfordandoxfordshire. com. Summer Mon-Sat 0930-1730, Sun 1000-1600, winter Mon-Sat 0930-1700, Sun 1000-1530*, provide an accommodation booking service.

History

Compared to many towns and cities in England, Oxford is not that old. There's no evidence of occupation in Roman times, although by then there was already a major road junction just to the north near Bicester. Even the Saxons probably only used the place as a river-crossing for their cattle, hence 'Oxenford', and never settled. In the late ninth century, though, King Alfred recognized the strategic importance of the gravelly banks at the confluence of the rivers Thames and Cherwell in defending his kingdom against the Danes. The town must have prospered, because the expected attack did come in 1009. The first Norman constable, Robert Doilly, built a castle overlooking the river in the west (of which one tower and the keep's mound survive) and ordered the construction of one of the first stone bridges in western Europe. **Folly Bridge**, completed in 1827, incorporating the Norman bridge beneath, is now a scheduled ancient monument. It wasn't until the late 12th century, when Henry II's wars with France prevented scholars from attending the University of Paris, that Oxford's position slap bang in the middle of England, well-connected to London and the rest of the country, made it a popular meeting place for informal gatherings of masters and wannabe masters. The South Range of Worcester College's main quad gives some idea of the houses these early academics favoured. Merton's Mob Quad is the oldest of the type of accommodation that they eventually adopted, although New College remains the most complete example of the hall, chapel and staircases later adopted by all colleges. The amazing Divinity School in the Bodleian Library was the first place to be owned by the university as a whole, before colleges were set up to safeguard the investments of benefactors. These religious foundations were dealt a hammer-blow by the Reformation but, thankfully, much of their architecture survived, making the city the best place in the country to explore Gothic and later neoclassical architecture. During the Civil War – which was fanned in part by the overhaul of the Church of England by Archbishop Laud of St John's College – Charles I based himself and his supporters at Christ Church. Come the Restoration, the university rose again, with illustrious alumni such as Christopher Wren (architect of the Sheldonian, Tom Tower and the Clarendon building) and the scientists Robert Boyle and Elias Ashmole. The 18th century was not a happy time in the university's history. Riddled with indolent Tories, it gained a reputation as as a marriage market for feckless aristos. The coming of the canal changed all that. The city expanded north, and today the spirit of Victorian Oxford and its industry can best be appreciated at the University Museum opposite the splendid red-brick confection of Keble College. In modern times, the Eagle Ironworks and Cowley car plant hugely increased the city's population. The suburbs in the north along the Banbury Road were for dons and their families, while Jericho was developed as affordable accommodation for artisans. East Oxford housed the workers in the car plant as it still just about does today.

West of Carfax

Most visitors using public transport approach central Oxford from the west. Walking up from the train station, the route up Hythe Bridge Street runs past the **Saïd Business School** (quite a sight in itself, with students perched at their terminals on display behind its glass front), over the Oxford Canal, and joins George Street at the junction of Worcester Street.

George Street continues gently uphill, past Gloucester Green bus station and market square on the left. The city meets the university proper 60 yards from the bus depot at the top of George Street where it hits Cornmarket. Most of the more interesting colleges are east of here, along Broad Street and the High Street (see East of Carfax, below).

One exception is **Worcester College**. A relatively young college, founded in 1714, its very grand 18th-century neoclassical buildings and lakeside garden surround the oldest example of scholars' accommodation in the city. The medieval South Range of the main quadrangle forms the adorably dinky remains of Gloucester College, a Benedictine monastery founded in 1283. Worcester Street heads north and becomes Walton Street, home to the **Ruskin Art School** (look out for degree shows by the most fashionable undergraduates at the university) and the Oxford University Press. The **Oxford University Press Museum** ① *Great Clarendon St, archives@oup.com, Mon-Fri 1000-1600 (not bank holidays) but book a time slot in advance, free*, has been recently refurbished. A little further down, between Walton Street and the canal, **Jericho** has long been one of the most happening parts of town (see Restaurants and Shopping below). At the top of Walton Street, Walton Well Road heads left down to **Port Meadow**, an amazingly unspoilt medieval watermeadow, still popular with skaters in winter, and frequented in the summer by grazing cows and undergraduates strolling over to pubs such as the *Perch* and the *Trout* on the river.

A right turn eastwards at the meeting of Worcester Street and Walton Street leads on to Beaumont Street. Here stands the Oxford Playhouse, which is opposite the **Ashmolean Museum** ① *Beaumont St, T01865-278000, www.ashmolean.org, Tue-Sun and bank holiday Mon 1000-1800, but check the website for early closure days, free*, the oldest museum open to the public in the country. It was opened early in the 17th century by Elias Ashmole, one of Charles I's tax-men. Today it ranks as one of the most extraordinary collections under one roof outside London. The grand classical façade hides more than 60 rooms, displaying art and archaeology from ancient times to the present day. The museum was totally refurbished in 2009, and the displays and galleries are now arranged around the theme 'Crossing Cultures, Crossing Time'. The best place to start is on the ground floor, home to the Ancient World exhibit. These rooms are full of artefacts from ancient Egypt, including the Princesses fresco from about 1340 BC, a fragment of delicate wall painting; artefacts from ancient Cyprus and Greece; artefacts from Rome, and Italy before Rome; from India, and ancient Chinese paintings. The first floor, Asian Crossroads, shifts forward in time and displays the museum's collection of Indian and Islamic art, showing the connections between Asia and the Mediterranean via trading routes. Moving up to the second floor, the East Meets West gallery is an impressive and extensive display of art and musical instruments from the Western world and from Japan and China, and includes pieces from the Italian Renaissance. Up to the next floor where gallery 3M displays the museum's collection of art from 1800 to the present day – a fantastic collection, including a whole room of Pissarro. Also on the third floor is the Special Exhibitions gallery; see the website for what's currently on display. Down in the basement are new galleries on Exploring the Past, along with the museum shop and café. Connected to the museum after a 2010 refurbishment is the **Cast Gallery** accessible from the Rome gallery on the ground floor, with an exceptional array of around 900 casts taken from Greek and Roman sculptures in other collections around the world.

With the Randolph Hotel on the corner, Beaumont Street meets the wide, tree-lined north–south thoroughfare of St Giles at the spikey **Martyrs Memorial**. It was erected in 1841 in memory of the Protestant bishops Cranmer, Ridley and Latimer who were burned at the stake during the counter-Reformation of 'Bloody Mary' in the mid-16th century. A cross marks the exact spot where their ashes were found outside Balliol College on the Broad (see below). Over the way is **St John's College**, consistently one of the highest academic achievers, with one of the most beautiful gardens in Oxford, fronted by a striking combination of Gothic and neoclassical architecture.

East of Carfax

The block of old streets and colleges formed by the Cornmarket, the Broad, Catte Street and the High Street is pretty much the heart of the university, embracing the University Church of St Mary the Virgin, the Radcliffe Camera, the Bodleian Library and Sheldonian Theatre, as well as Jesus, Exeter and Brasenose colleges.

Cornmarket itself may not be the most inspiring street in the centre, but it conceals some hidden gems. The small **Painted Room** ① *3 Cornmarket (above Republic and hidden by an 18th-century façade)*, is where Shakespeare is supposed to have stayed when in town. The bard was apparently godfather to the son of the keeper of the Crown Inn that once stood on this site, John Davenant. Wooden panels on one wall slide back to reveal some remarkable Tudor wall painting, with white Canterbury bells, windflowers, roses and even a passion flower interlaced in the twisting design. The Oxford Preservation Trust are currently negotiating access with the owners, Oxford City Council, so access is limited, but contact the Trust on T01865-242918 for up-to-date information on visits. Behind is the **Covered Market**, now faintly twee but nonetheless another unusual survivor and an 18th-century precursor to modern shopping malls, currently occupied by some tempting permanent stalls. It's a great spot for buying picnic foods in the summer (see Shopping, page 73). On the way through from Cornmarket, more expansive but perhaps less significant medieval wall paintings can be seen behind glass on the walls of the local **Pizza Express**, re-named the **Golden Cross Restaurant** in honour of the inn that once stood here. At the top of the Cornmarket, the Saxon **tower of St Michael's** ① *T01865-255776, summer daily 1030-1700, winter daily 1030-1600*, at the North Gate, on the corner of Ship Street, was built in about 1040, allowing it to be dubbed the 'oldest building in Oxford', although the rest of the church is 13th century. The view from the top, reached via displays on the history of the church and some large bells, is definitely worth the climb.

A right turn at the end of Cornmarket heads into the Broad, perhaps the archetypical university street. Located here is **Balliol College**, not much to look at but one of the university's more radical powerhouses. Next door, **Trinity** has an unassuming cottage for a porter's lodge instead of the usual grand gatehouse, but the college's beauties include a late-17th-century chapel with carved limewood and juniper screen by Grinling Gibbons, and Wren's lovely Garden Quad, the first neoclassical building in the university.

Opposite Trinity, in the splendid late 17th-century building that once housed the Ashmolean, the **Museum of the History of Science** ① *Broad St, T01865-277280, www. mhs.ox.ac.uk, Tue-Fri 1200-1700, Sat 1000-1700, Sun 1400-1700, free*, displays a fascinating and old-fashioned collection of scientific landmarks: early chemical stills, chronometers, the original apparatus for manufacturing penicillin and Islamic and European astrolabes.

Next door, the **Sheldonian Theatre** ① *Broad St, T01865-277299, www.ox.ac.uk/ sheldonian, Mar-Oct 1000-1230 and 1400-1630; Nov-Feb 1400-1530 (subject to university events), £2.50, concessions £1.50*, is the university's hall of ceremonies, also designed by Wren, who studied astronomy nearby at All Souls. Its ceiling is painted with the triumph of Truth, allied with Arts and Sciences, over Ignorance. An octagonal rooftop cupola above provides sheltered wraparound views of that famous skyline come wind or rain.

Its neighbour, the **Clarendon Building**, was constructed by Wren's pupil Hawksmoor to the plans of Vanbrugh, architect of Blenheim Palace, as a printing house. Now it makes a grand front door for the **Bodleian Library** ⓘ *Broad St, T01865-277000, www.bodley. ox.ac.uk, Mon-Fri 0900-1700, Sat 0900-1630, Sun 1100-1700 (subject to university events); no children under 11; tours range from £2.50 to £13 and last from 30 to 90 mins; access to the Divinity School £1; first come, first serve on all tickets except the extended tour,* the university's chief academic resource and one of the greatest, certainly the oldest public libraries in the world. Its extraordinary Gothic Jacobean central courtyard has to be seen to be believed. Through the glass doors on the right, the 15th-century Divinity School is the oldest part of the building, with a magnificent vaulted stone ceiling, and served as the Infirmary in the Harry Potter films. The library itself is one of the wonders of the western world; its most ancient room, the mysterious and magical Duke Humfrey's Library was also used in the Harry Potter films, as Hogwarts library.

The library makes up the north side of Radcliffe Square, effectively the centre of the university, with 18th-century Scottish architect James Gibbs' majestic domed **Radcliffe Camera** plonked unceremoniously in the middle. Originally intended as a medical library, it now houses the English literature, film studies and history sections of the Bodleian library and is closed to the public. On the south side of the square, the **University Church of St Mary** seals the university off from the High Street behind. The church itself has a long history of ecclesiastical wrangling, but most visitors come for the climb up the **tower** ⓘ *T01865-279111, Mon-Sat 0900-1700, Sun 1145-1700 (Jul, Aug until 1800), last admission 30 mins before closing, £4, children £3,* to overlook the Radcliffe Camera. It's probably the best viewpoint (and the highest) in the centre of the city. Round on the High Street side, the barley-sugar columns and broken pediment of the original church porch were possibly inspired by a Raphael cartoon in the collection of Charles I.

Nathaniel Hawthorne described the High Street as the "noblest old street in England", an impression confirmed now that it's virtually traffic-free apart from buses. It curves round to the south, with the postgraduate college **All Souls** (the 15th-century stained glass and oak roof of its chapel can be inspected on request) on the left, facing **University College**, not the oldest but certainly one of the most academic colleges. Next door, over Logic Lane, are the Victorian Examination Schools, still in use, opposite **Queen's College** which occupies flamboyant Baroque buildings. A left turn beyond leads up narrow Queens Lane, past the medieval **St Edmund Hall** into New College Lane, which is lined with famous gargoyles and twists around beneath the mock **'Bridge of Sighs'** back to the Broad. **New College** is famous for its chapel, hall and cloisters, and for its beautiful gardens, which are dominated by the old city wall and a viewing mound supposedly marking the site of a plague pit.

Back on the High Street, continuing south, the **Botanic Gardens** ⓘ *T01865-286690, Nov-Feb 0900-1600, Mar/Apr and Sep/Oct 0900-1700, May-Aug 0900-1800, last entry 45 mins before close, £4.50, concessions £3, children free,* are on the right beyond Rose Lane, sheltering behind high walls and ornate Jacobean stone gates. The oldest of their kind in Britain (dating from 1621), they evolved from an apothecary's herb garden into this well-labelled horticultural wonderland, with tropical glasshouses, a walled garden and charming riverside walks. Rose Lane leads into **Christ Church meadow**, Oxford's answer to Cambridge's 'backs'.

Over the road, next to its bridge and beneath its unmistakable perpendicular tower, stands **Magdalen** (pronounced *Maudlin*) **College**, the most spread-out and gloriously sited of all the old colleges. The medieval chapel, hall and cloisters should be seen, but the highlight is the so-called New Building of 1733, an elegant neoclassical edifice standing in its very own deer park close by the confluence of the rivers Thames (or 'Isis' as it's called in Oxford) and Cherwell (pronounced *Char-wool*).

Southeast from here down **Cowley Road** is the pavement jewellery trail, a set of 58 ingots set into the pavement which form a puzzle which explains the history and evolution of this road.

Museums and parks

The wide green expanse of the **University Parks** to the north of the city centre are the destination of many a leisurely punt up from Magdalen Bridge or down from the Cherwell Boathouse. The parks also border a couple of museums. The **University Museum of Natural History** ① *Parks Rd, T01865-272950, www.oum.ox.ac.uk*, is unfortunately closed throughout 2013 for roof repairs, but check the website for details of how to see the collection via it's behind-the-scenes tours.

Just behind, the **Pitt Rivers Museum** ① *South Parks Rd, T01865-270927, www.prm.ox.ac. uk, Mon 1200-1630, Tue-Sun 1000-1630, free*, displays the university's anthropological and ethnographic collections in a famously fusty Victorian way: slide open draws to discover African charms and Inuit ornaments, and peer through glass cases at shrunken heads and Native American scalps. Children love it. Over the road from the museums, another Victorian marvel is the stripy red-brick and stone **Keble College**, where Holman Hunt's *Light of the World* in the chapel is the main attraction.

South of Carfax

Carfax Tower on the south side of the crossroads is all that remains of St Martin's Church, once the parish church of the city. The name Carfax derives from the Latin *quadri furcus* (four-forked), and indeed it was the church's position on such a busy crossroads that necessitated its demolition in 1896. The view south from **Carfax Tower** ① *daily 1000-1730, closes 1630 in Oct, £2.30, children £1.20*, is dominated by Wren's imposing gatehouse for Christ Church College, topped by Tom Tower.

Christ Church ① *T01865-276492, www.chch.ox.ac.uk, check the website for opening times and note that the college is often closed 1140-1430, last admission 1630, £7, children & concessions £5.50, family £14*, is the largest, most spectacular and most commercialized of the colleges. It was founded by Cardinal Wolsey (hence 'Cardinal College' in Hardy's *Jude the Obscure*) and re-founded by Henry VIII after his break with Rome; he saved some money by making its chapel the city's cathedral. The college is the university's largest and in Tom Quad you know it. Used by Royalists in the Civil War as a cattlepen, during the 18th century it became famous for the antics of its equally bovine aristocratic undergraduates or 'junior members' as they're known at 'the House'. Tom Quad, the cathedral and the picture gallery are well worth a look round. The **cathedral** ① *T01865-276155*, is the country's smallest and contains the recently restored shrine of the city's patron saint, St Frideswide, as well as some beautiful pre-Reformation stained glass, including an unusual depiction of the murder of St Thomas à Becket which survived because the martyr's head was replaced with plain glass. His face is still missing. Look out too for the illustration in the south transept of Osney Abbey, long since vanished. The **picture gallery** ① *accessed via Canterbury Gate, but you can enter from Oriel Sq if you are not in Christ Church, T01865-276172, Oct-May Mon, Wed & Sat 1030-1300 and 1400-1630, Sun 1400-1630, Jun Mon, Wed and Sat 1030-1700, Sun 1400-1700, Jul-Sep Mon-Sat 1030-1700, Sun 1400-1700, £3, concessions £2*, housed in a purpose-built modernist block sunk next to the library, is particularly famous for its collection of Old Master drawings.

These include the translucent beauty of Verrochio's *Head of a Young Woman* from the late 15th century, Bellini's *Portrait of a Man* and Leonardo's *Grotesque Head*, as well as works by Raphael, Durer, Titian, Rubens and Lorrain. The paintings on display include a 14th-century triptych, Tintoretto's *Portrait of a Gentleman*, Hals' *Portrait of a Woman* and Veronese's *Mystic Marriage of St Catherine*. One of the gallery's charms is the way that it has maintained intact the different tastes of its four major benefactors. As well as 13 future prime ministers, the Elizabethan soldier, courtier and poet Sir Philip Sydney, Robert Burton, author of *The Anatomy of Melancholy*, the poet and playwright Ben Jonson, art historian John Ruskin and archaeologist William Buckland, probably the college's most famous alumnus is Charles Lutteridge Dodgson, aka Lewis Carroll, the author of *Alice in Wonderland*. The garden gate behind the cathedral that supposedly inspired the mathematician's story has become something of a shrine.

Just up the hill from Christ Church on St Aldate's, the **Town Hall and Museum of Oxford** ① *St Aldate's, T01865-252351, Mon-Sat 1000-1700, Sun 1100-1500, free*, recently relocated into the town hall, gives the full low-down on the history of the city and its people with interactive activities for past and present. Off to the right down Pembroke Street, **Modern Art Oxford** ① *30 Pembroke St, T01865-722733, www.modernartoxford.org.uk, Tue and Wed 1000-1700, Thu-Sat 1000-1900, Sun 1200-1700, free*, is the city's top place for exhibitions of internationally respected contemporary art. A barn-like space, it's particularly suitable for large works and has a well-stocked bookshop attached.

West of Oxford → *For listings, see pages 69-74.*

Although the Thames actually enters Oxford from the north, its broad valley dominates the area west of the city. Meandering through open countryside, sometimes marred by pylons and reservoirs, the river gives this part of the country its special quality. The largest town, the old market centre of Witney, in fact straddles the River Windrush, one of the most charming of the Thames' tributaries. Descending from the Cotswold hills, the Windrush passes through the beautiful honey-coloured town of Burford, famously the 'gateway to the Cotswolds'. Then it winds through peaceful villages such as Asthall, past the romantic ruined manor house at Minster Lovell, before finding the Thames just beyond Stanton Harcourt. Here a complete medieval estate is still inhabited by descendants of the Harcourt family. Further up the Thames, meanwhile, on opposite banks of the river, are two remarkable places associated with left-wing pioneers of very different types. The 16th-century manor house at Kelmscott was the delightful summer retreat of William Morris in late Victorian times, while the grey classical pile at Burcot witnessed the antics of some exotic Labour-leaning socialites and thinkers in the 1930s.

Arriving in the west of Oxford
Getting there The A40 **road** heads west from north Oxford via Witney (10 miles) and Burford (17 miles) towards Cheltenham and Gloucester. It intersects with major roads running north–south at both Witney and Burford. **Stagecoach** ① *T01865-772250*, runs the S1 service from Oxford, which goes via Witney, and the S2, which goes to Witney and Minster Lovell. There are also buses to Burford. Other services link Lechlade with Cirencester and Swindon. ▸▸ *For further details, see Transport, page 74.*

Information Witney TIC ① *3 Welch Way, T01993-775802, daily 0900-1730.* **Burford TIC** ① *33a High St, T01993-823558, Mon-Sat 0930-1700, Sun 1000-1600*

Upper Thames and Windrush valleys

The Thames runs south into Oxford. But going against the stream north and west out of the city, past Port Meadow, Godstow and some old abbey ruins, and heading west just south of the A40, the river skirts **Wytham Great Wood**. These 600 acres or so of deciduous hilltop woodland have been carefully managed by the university and now provide a habitat for all manner of rare north European birds, including nightingales, warblers and also a heronry. **Eynsham**, three miles west of the city ring road, was an important medieval town, a fact still reflected in its market square and old town hall. A mile south, at **Swinford**, the fine 18th-century bridge over the river operates the oldest and cheapest toll in the country. A couple more miles west, north of the Thames and east of the Windrush, **Stanton Harcourt** is a peaceful little grey-stone village. The surprisingly grand Norman cruciform church features one of the oldest screens in the country (13th-century) and a massive collection of monuments to the Harcourt family dating from the 12th century until the early 18th. Next door, their **manor house** ① *T01865-881928, Apr-Sep limited opening 1400-1800, please call for details*, was described by Alexander Pope as "the true picture of a genuine Ancient Country Seat," high praise from the greatest satirical poet of the Enlightenment, but then he was translating Homer's *Iliad* in the top of the tower here (open by appointment), in 1718. As well as 12 acres of gardens, complete with medieval fish and stew ponds, the old kitchen and private chapel are both very interesting.

Witney and around

Bypassed by the A40, the old market town of Witney has an attractive centre and splendid church. Just to its north, off the A4095, the **Cogges Manor Farm Museum** ① *Church Lane, T01993-772602, Farm Mar-Nov Tue-Sun 1100-1700, £4, children £3; manor house Sat, Sun and bank holidays, £5.50, children £4*, is worth the short detour. This attractive farmstead was reopened in 2011, showing small-scale and sustainable farming and how Cogges Farm has developed since Saxon times.

Three miles west of Witney, **Minster Lovell Hall and Dovecote** ① *(EH) usually Oct-Mar 1000-1600, free*, is a picturesque, ruined 15th-century manor house in a pleasant spot on the banks of the river Windrush, alongside an ancient dovecote.

Heading back towards the river, six miles south of Witney, **Bampton** is where Morris dancing is supposed to have originated, hence perhaps the unusually large number of pubs in the old town and also the unusually large number of men who enjoy them. The road south off the B4449 crosses the Thames at **Tadpole Bridge**, where there's a tiny campsite at Rushey Lock (not accessible by car) on one of the most unspoiled stretches of the river, and a pub, **The Trout Inn**.

Six miles west of Tadpole, **Kelmscott Manor** ① *T01367-252486, Apr-Oct Wed and Sat 1100-1700 (tickets available from 1030), £9, under-16s and students £4.50, garden only £2.50*, is a very fine 16th-century house hidden behind high walls in a quiet out-of-the-way village, where the great Socialist William Morris summered from 1871 until his death in 1896. He shared it with the pre-Raphaelite poet Gabriel Dante Rossetti. The place has been restored and preserved by the Society of Antiquaries as a home for a considerable collection of Morris's works – furniture, textiles and ceramics – in his highly influential, flowery (and usually poorly imitated) neo-medievalist style. Overall, a visit here confirms what Morris believed – that a great opportunity was lost during the industrial revolution to beautify the world with mass-production rather than cheapen it.

A walk west along the Thames Path from Kelmscott passes **Buscot Weir** and the National Trust village of Buscot, with its inevitable teashop; there are pleasant walks further along the river to the old Cheese Wharf. A mile or so east of Buscot village, **Buscot Park** ① (NT), T01367-240786, www.buscot-park.com, Mar-Sep 1400-1800, check website for days, £8, children £4, grounds only £5, was once famous as the weekend retreat of the left-wing thinkers, artists and poets that gathered around Gavin Henderson, Lord Faringdon, in the 1930s. An austere, late-18th-century house, it contains the Faringdon Collection, a particularly impressive art collection, including works by Rubens and Rembrandt and Burne-Jones's *Legend of the Briar Rose*, Sleeping Beauty to most of us. Upstairs, there are some remarkable English paintings of the 19th and 20th centuries by the likes of Gainsborough, Reynolds and Graham Sutherland. The spectacular Italianate water garden was laid out by Harold Peto in the early 20th century. On the way to it, the east pavilion is decorated with murals depicting the heady revolutionary fervour of the dinner parties held at the house.

Lechlade and around
Three miles northwest of Buscot, Lechlade on Thames (actually in a little pocket of Gloucestershire) is the highest navigable point on the river, and consequently a Mecca for pleasure cruisers. Best seen from the old St John's Bridge, next to yet another **Trout Inn** (see below), the spire of **St Lawrence's church** rises above the trees while the river snakes lazily across the meadows. The mainly 16th-century church inspired Shelley's *Stanzas in a Summer Evening Churchyard* on his boating trip up to Lechlade in 1815. The town itself comes as a bit of a disappointment, with its slightly desperate antique shops and poky little cafés, but nonetheless has a welcoming and friendly attitude, well-accustomed as it is to a stream of strangers messing about in boats.

Lechlade is also an important road junction. The A361 heads south from here for 10 miles to Swindon and north for nine miles to Burford, crossing the A417 Wantage–Cirencester road. Five miles towards Burford, beyond a perfectly preserved 18th-century watermill at **Little Faringdon**, the **Swinford Museum** ① Filkins, near Lechlade, T01367-860331, 1st Sun of May-Sep 1430-1700, free, is one of the oldest small museums in Oxfordshire and contains a collection of domestic and agricultural tools housed in a 17th-century cottage.

Three miles further up the road to Burford, the **Cotswold Wildlife Park** ① T01993-823006, www.cotswoldwildlifepark.co.uk, Apr-Oct daily 1000-1800 (last admission 1630), Nov-Mar daily 1000-1700 or dusk (last admission 1530), £14, children £9.50, is set in acres of fine parkland around a Victorian manor house. It's a hugely popular local attraction where zebras and rhinos can be seen roaming their generous enclosures from the picnic lawns, while a miniature steam railway chugs around in the summer months. As well as caring for some endangered red pandas, the zoo also takes its gardening seriously, with a tropical house, 'hot bed' and walled garden.

Burford
Since its decline as an important medieval wool town, Burford has long billed itself as the 'Gateway to the Cotswolds' and strikingly lovely and stone-built it is too. That's no secret though, which means that during the summer months the gate pressure can be intense: the long broad High Street, sloping down to the old bridge over the little river Windrush, becomes impossibly busy. Even so, the crush in the antique shops, pubs and tearooms can easily be avoided on the smaller side streets. One such, at the lower end of the High Street, leads to Burford's **church of St John**, the most outstanding parish church in the county. Its Norman tower has survived, later topped with a spire, and the medieval warren of arches, chapels, nooks and crannies inside should definitely not be missed. The church

has some intriguing monuments, including one to Henry VIII's hairdresser that features the first known depiction of a native South American in England. Another carving is a possible likeness of a fertility goddess from the second century. The font bears the scratched name of one of the mutinous Levellers imprisoned here by Oliver Cromwell for three nights in 1649. On 17 May, three of them were executed, an event still commemorated in the town on the nearest Saturday to that date with some fancy dress and not-so-fancy politicizing.

The town itself has retained, virtually unaltered, its medieval street plan. Originally, the main road ran east–west past the 16th-century market hall, called the **Tolsey** (now housing a local history museum); there are still several houses around it that bear traces of the Middle Ages. From the bridge, a very pleasant walk follows the banks of the Windrush eastwards for about three miles to the village of **Swinbrook**, where there's another church with remarkable tombs inside and the graves of Nancy and Unity Mitford outside.

Half a mile away to the north, at **Widford** is a tiny church in an even more idyllic setting and incorporating the remains of a Roman villa. The pretty and relatively undiscovered village of **Asthall**, a mile further downstream, is also well worth a visit. Another riverside walk heads west along the Windrush to **Taynton**, and a couple of miles further to **Great Barrington**, where **The Fox Inn** does excellent lunches and has accommodation (see below).

Oxfordshire listings

For hotel and restaurant price codes and other relevant information, see pages 9-12.

● Where to stay

Oxford *p57, map p58*
Hotels in Oxford are generally expensive for what you get, and hotels in the lower price brackets are almost non-existent although there are lots of B&Bs on Abingdon Rd and Banbury Rd. There are hardly enough affordable rooms for students in the city, so visitor accommodation is at a premium and you should book well in advance, especially in the summer. The TIC runs the usual booking service, but don't expect to be within walking distance of the sights if you leave it too late.

If you are visiting during university holidays, a great budget option is to stay in one of the colleges, from £30 a night B&B. Check www.oxfordrooms.co.uk to see what is available.

££££ The Macdonald Randolph, Beaumont St, T01865-256400, www.macdonaldhotels.co.uk. Landmark building in the city centre, home to the **Morse Bar** – recognizable as the bar of choice for Inspector Morse in the TV series.

££££ Malmaison Oxford, Oxford Castle, 3 New Rd, T0844-693 0659, www.malmaison.com. A former prison that is now a boutique hotel. It's the rooms that are the real pull of this hotel: luxurious and original.

££££ Old Parsonage Hotel, 1 Banbury Rd, T01865-310210, www.oldparsonage-hotel.co.uk. Formerly Oscar Wilde's undergraduate digs and now one of the poshest hotels in town, run by the same people as Gee's Restaurant. Building dates back to 1660. Complimentary walking tours and bicycles available to guests.

£££ The Burlington House, 374 Banbury Rd, T01865-513513, www.burlington-hotel-oxford.co.uk. Charming and welcoming little boutique B&B some distance up the

Banbury Rd, but there are plenty of buses. Very good breakfast.

£££ Head of the River, Folly Bridge, St Aldate's, T01865-721600, www.headoftheriveroxford.co.uk. Large Fuller's pub and hotel overlooking river to the south. Breakfast included.

£££ Old Bank Hotel, 92-94 High St, T01865-799599, www.oldbank-hotel.co.uk. One of the most stylish and central places to stay in the city. 42 individual rooms (likely to have good views of the famous skyline) and the **Quod Bar and Grill**, a stylish brasserie-type place with a sunny outdoor drinking deck in summer. Also offers free walking tours and bicycles to guests.

£££ Remont Oxford, 367 Banbury Rd, T01865-311020, www.remont-oxford.co.uk. Again, a little further away from the centre but easy to get the bus into town. This B&B has recently been refurbished to a hotel standard and is clean, spacious and chic.

£££-££ The Tower House, 15 Ship St, T01865-246828, www.oxfordhotelsandinns.com. Bang in the middle of town, in a 17th-century house, tucked away off Cornmarket, with 7 rooms.

££ Acorn Guest House, 260 Iffley Rd, T01865-247998, www.oxford-acorn.co.uk. Four comfortable double rooms, a 20-min walk into town. Similar in price and style to many of the B&Bs strung out along the main road into town from the south and east.

££ Green Gables Guest House, 326 Abingdon Rd, T01865-725870, www.greengables.uk.com. Offers 7 double rooms, fairly clean and comfortable, with breakfast; some way out town near Donnington Bridge.

£ The Backpackers Hostel, 9a Hythe Bridge St, T01865-721761, www.hostels.co.uk. Close to the station, and has 10 bunkrooms for 4-10 people each. Open 24 hrs.

£ YHA Hostel, 2a Botley Rd, T0845-371 9131. Just behind the railway station, this hostel can be reached from the westbound platform through a little alleyway. It is fairly smart with 180 beds in dorms and rooms. Open 24 hrs.

Camping

The Camping and Caravanning Club, 426 Abingdon Rd, on the ring-road south of Oxford, 1.5 miles from city centre. T0845-130 7633. Open all year, 129 sites.

West of Oxford p65

££££ Burford House Hotel, 99 High St, Burford, T01993-823151, www.burford-house.co.uk. In a stunning 17th-century building, this family-run hotel has plenty of friendly touches and a pleasant easy-going atmosphere.

££££ The Lamb, Sheep St, Burford, T01993-823155, www.cotswold-inns-hotels.co.uk. The former home of Sir Lawrence Tanfield, Lord Chief Baron of the Exchequer in the reign of Queen Elizabeth I, offers log fires, flagstone floors and real ales. Rooms are quiet and individually furnished in a comforting style. The fairly expensive restaurant does top-notch food, and there are sandwiches and deli boards at the bar.

££££ Old Swan & Minster Mill, Minster Lovell, T01993-774441, www.oldswanandminstermill.com. There are historical rooms and a gastro-pub in the **Old Swan**, with more modern (and modest) rooms next door in Minster Mill. Dog-friendly, for an extra charge.

£££ The Angel at Burford, Witney St, Burford, T01993-822714, www.theangelatburford.co.uk. A very highly rated pub-restaurant offering a gastro-pub style menu and spacious yet cosy double rooms.

£££ Bay Tree Hotel Sheep St, Burford, T01993-822791, www.cotswold-inns-hotels.co.uk. Wysteria-clad on the outside, chintzy within. Very comfortable, with a reputable restaurant.

£££ The Fox Inn, Great Barrington, near Burford, T01451-844385, www.foxinnbarrington.com. A very good pint can be had in this charming riverside pub with a garden. There's some very decent English

country cooking 7 days a week and 3 rooms with bathroom en suite.

££ The Ferryman Inn, Bablock Hythe, Northmoor, T01865-880028, www.theferrymaninn.co.uk. Closed Tue. A couple of miles from Stanton Harcourt, this famous waterside freehouse offers a ferry service across the river, simple but well-equipped rooms, pub grub and a very cheery atmosphere.

££ Rectory Farm, Northmoor, nr Witney, T01865-300207, www.oxtowns.co.uk/rectoryfarm. 2 B&B rooms are available in a very fine early 17th-century stone farmhouse that once belonged to St John's College, Oxford. Self-catering holiday cottages also available.

❼ Restaurants

Oxford p57, map p58

A lot of Oxford's trendy bars, cafés and restaurants rated by the locals are found off the Cowley Rd; the pricier establishments can be found in the centre of town. The other option for food as well as booze is one of the pubs (see below), even though they can sometimes become too lively to make eating a pleasure.

£££ Gee's Restaurant and Bar, 61 Banbury Rd, T01865-553540, www.gees-restaurant.co.uk. Enjoy your lunch in the newly renovated iconic glasshouse, originally used for growing vegetables in the 1890s.

£££-££ Brasserie Blanc, 71-72 Walton St, T01865-510999, www.brasserieblanc.com. Brasserie-style dishes at Raymond Blanc's chain; many think it's not particularly good value for money – the set menu is a better bang for your buck.

££ Branca Restaurant & Bar, 111 Walton St, T01865-556111, www.branca.co.uk. Popular, modern Italian restaurant, with a traditional menu, often very busy with a lively atmosphere.

££ The Cherwell Boathouse, Bardwell Rd, T01865-552746, www.cherwellboathouse.co.uk. Have a fine lunchtime feast in a clapperboard hut, then hire a punt. Or enjoy a more expensive and leisurely supper on the waterside.

££ Edamame, 15 Holywell St, T01865-246916, www.edamame.co.uk. Highly rated Japanese restaurant serving authentic dishes. No reservations, but worth the wait if there is a queue (there often is). Open for lunch Wed-Sun; for sushi on Thu evenings and also open for evening dining on Fri and Sat.

££ Golden Cross Pizza Express, Golden Cross Inn, off the Cornmarket, T01865-790442, www.pizzaexpress.com. Heavily restored in 1988 (see page 62). A good fall-back.

££ Moya, 97 St Clements St, T01865-200111, www.moya-oxford.biz. Traditional Slovak food with generous portions. Also serves as a cocktail bar.

££ Pierre Victoire Bistrot, 9 Little Clarendon St, T01865-316616, www.pierrevictoire.co.uk. Vibrant French bistro serving traditional food to expectant diners.

££-£ Al-Shami, 25 Walton Cres, T01865-310066, www.al-shami.co.uk. This restaurant has now been here 25 years and offers some superior Lebanese cuisine, with a particularly good mezze selection.

£ Atomic Burger, 96 Cowley Rd, T01865-790855, www.atomicburger.co.uk. May not have the best burgers in the world but does have a great, unusual menu, and the retro comic-book theme is fun.

£ The Gardeners Arms, 39 Plantation Rd, T01865-559814, www.thegarden-oxford.co.uk. Hearty vegetarian food.

£ Kazbar, 25-27 Cowley Rd, T01865-202920, www.kazbar.co.uk. Spanish and North African restaurant offering tasty tapas.

£ Malikas, 218 Cowley Rd, T01865-723029, www.malikasrestaurant.co.uk. An excellent contemporary Indian restaurant with a modern dining room.

£ Peppers Burgers, 84 Walton St, T01865-511592, www.peppersburgers.com. The pure beef burgers have been a hit with students for the last 25 years. Some say the best takeaway burger in Oxford is to be found here. Also does pizza.

£ SoJo, 6-9 Hythe Bridge St, T01865-202888, www.sojooxford.co.uk. Down by the station, no-frills, authentic Chinese food. Very highly rated by the locals.

Cafés

Grand Café, 84 High St, T01865-204463. Claims to be the oldest coffeehouse in England. Charming service and high prices for some superb cafetière coffees, American-style sandwiches and light meals.

Jericho Café, 112 Walton St, T01865-310840. A popular haunt for brunch.

The Missing Bean, Turl St, T01865-794886. Locally roasted Brazilian coffee, good ciabatta sarnies and a wide selection of home-baked cakes and pastries.

Quarter Horse Coffee, Cowley Rd, T01865-428808. Great coffee and great teas.

Queen's Lane Coffee House, 40 High St, T01865-240082. Also claiming to be the oldest coffeehouse in town, this place has been serving since 1654. Turkish coffee available, plus an extensive lunch menu.

The Rose, 51 High St, T01865-244429. A bright, refurbished little café with an imaginative menu and lovely afternoon teas.

Zappi's Bike Café, 28-32 St Michaels St, www.zappisbikecafe.com. A really friendly venue that serves up good coffee and home-made cakes.

West of Oxford *p65*

See also Where to stay, above, and Pubs, bars and clubs, below.

£££ The Trout Inn, Tadpole Bridge, Lechlade on Thames, T01367-252313, www.trout-inn.co.uk. This busy waterside oasis does good food and also has rooms available (**£££**).

££ Mermaid Inn, High St, Burford, T01993-822193, www.themermaidburford.co.uk. A very old building, with decent-enough pub grub.

££ The Royal Oak, Ramsden, near Witney, T01993-868213, www.royaloakramsden.com.

A freehouse that does very good food. Ramsden is a quiet village located on Akeman St, the Roman road that connected Bicester and Cirencester.
££ The Swan Inn, Swinbrook, T01993-823339, www.theswanswinbrook.co.uk, near the Windrush. A very old pub, where the food's all home-made and locally sourced, and the ales are well-kept.

Cafés
£ The Priory Tearoom, High St, Burford, T01993-823249. Good breakfasts and afternoon teas.

Pubs, bars and clubs

Oxford *p57, map p58*
Oxonians are understandably proud of the city's pubs.
The Bear, 6 Alfred St, T01865-728264, www.bearoxford.co.uk. A cosy, wood-panelled old pub popular with the local Christ Church students and also with rugby union clubs from around the world, judging by the array of old ties in the back bar. Not for tall people (ie anyone over 5ft 5). Good for cask ales.
Café Tarifa, Cowley Rd, T01865-256091, www.cafe-tarifa.co.uk. A relaxed cocktail bar with a Mediterranean/North African vibe and live music.
Duke of Cambridge, 5-6 Little Clarendon St, T01865-558173, www.dukebar.com. A popular and lively cocktail bar.
Eagle and Child, St Giles, T01865-302925, www.nicholsonspubs.co.uk. Known as the 'Bird and Baby', this is another cosy place to drink. It was once the favourite haunt of 'the Inklings', JRR Tolkien and CS Lewis.
The House, Blue Boar St, T01865-724433, www.housebar.co.uk. Buzzing cocktail bar with a great terrace and a games room.
King's Arms, on the corner of Holywell St and Broad St, T01865-242369, www.youngs.co.uk. Some good Young's beer but quite expensive grub. Popular with students.
The Perch, Binsey, T01865-728891, www.the-perch.co.uk, Wed-Sun only.

A little out of town but makes for a pleasant walk across Port Meadow and has a tree-shaded riverside garden.
Raoul's Bar, 32 Walton St, T01865-553732, www.raoulsbar.co.uk. Cocktail bar with an impressive menu.
The Trout Inn, Lower Wolvercote, T01865-510930, www.thetroutoxford.co.uk. Beside an old bridge and weir.
Turf Tavern, beyond Bath Pl off Holywell La. Yet another real ale pub, with reasonable pub grub served up all day to heaving crowds outside, beneath the old city wall of New College, and inside in the snug, low-ceilinged bars.

Clubs
Surprisingly short on good nightspots, Oxford's clubs come and go.
The Bridge, 6-9 Hythe Bridge St, T01865-242526, www.bridgeoxford.co.uk. Student nights in the week, but the club is over-21s only on Sat.
Lava & Ignite, Cantay House, Park End St, T01865-250181,www.lavaignite.com/oxford. A large venue with a spectrum of pop, dance and R'n'B.
Roppongi, 29 George St, T01865-241574, www.roppongioxford.com. One of the latest uber-cool offerings, marketing itself as chic, upmarket and elite.

West of Oxford *p65*
See also Where to stay and Restaurants, above.
The Bell, Ducklington, near Witney, T01993-702514, www.thebellinnducklington.co.uk. A thatched pub that has lovely flowers outside and traditional pub games, such as 'Aunt Sally', inside.
The Plough Inn, Kelmscott, T01367-253543, www.theploughinnkelmscott.com. A gorgeous little village pub with a wide selection of real ales.
White Hart Inn, Wytham, near the River Thames and the A34, T01865-244372, www.whitehartwytham.co.uk. Heated barn for winter surrounded by flowerbeds, situated on a quiet backroad.

☻ Entertainment

Oxford *p57, map p58*
Cinema
Odeon, Magdalen St, and **Odeon**, George St, T0871-224 4007, are the mainstream screens in the centre of town. **The Phoenix**, Walton St, T01865-512526, www.picturehouses.co.uk, shows mainstream and arthouse films and is inevitably a much nicer experience. The **Ultimate Picture Palace**, Jeune St, Cowley Rd, T01865-245288, www.uppcinema.co.uk, is a lovely independent cinema that shows arthouse, mainstream and classic movies.

Theatre and comedy venues
Burton Taylor Studio. Part of the Oxford Playhouse (see below), just next door. For innovative, new and fringe productions.
The Glee Club, Hythe Bridge St, T0871-472 0400, www.glee.co.uk/oxford. Comedy club and music venue, Fri and Sat.
New Theatre Oxford, George St, T01865-320760. Large-scale touring productions, musicals, operas and pantomimes.
Oxford Playhouse, Beaumont St, T01865-305305, www.oxfordplayhouse.com. The main theatre for drama and middle-scale touring productions by the likes of the National Theatre and Almeida Theatre Company.

☻ Shopping

Oxford *p57, map p58*
High St is a haven for independent shops and boutiques, including **Sanders of Oxford**, at No.104, a fascinating shop selling maps and fine prints; **Aspire**, which has an gorgeous collection of accessories, jewellery and gifts, and the **University of Oxford Shop**, at No.106, which does all those monogrammed sweatshirts and souvenirs to show the folks back home. Little Clarendon St is the place for gift shops and funky home furnishings, while Broad St is the place to go for bookshops and

art galleries. **The Old Fire Station Shop**, 40 George St, is a treasure trove of wares created by local artists and designers.

Books
Blackwell's, 48-51 Broad St, T01865-792792. The University booksellers, with an excellent second-hand section as well as all the latest new and academic titles.
Waterfield's, 52 High St, T01865-721809. An interesting second-hand and antiquarian bookseller.
Waterstone's, Broad St, T01865-790212.

Markets
For picnic materials, the **Covered Market** is home to: **Ben's Cookies**, T01865-247407, for huge, gooey delicious cookies in a variety of flavours; **Cake Shop** for cakes, biscuits and sweet decorations as well as doughs, and **Pieminister** for delicious pies made with quality ingredients.

☻ What to do

Oxford *p57, map p58*
Boating
Punts can be hired from **Cherwell Boathouse**, off Bardwell Rd, T01865-515978; **Magdalen Bridge Boat House**, Magdalen Bridge, T01865-202643, and **Salter's Steamers**, Folly Bridge, T01865-243421, www.salterssteamers.co.uk, who also run boat trips on the Thames. **College Cruisers**, Combe Rd Wharf, Combe Rd, T01865-554343, www.collegecruisers.com, hire out cruising boats on the river by the week.

Walking
Official guided tours leave from the TIC, where there are also some good self-guiding leaflets available on walks along the river or canal and around the town. The Oxford Canal walk runs all the way up to Coventry, on level ground, through picturesque countryside. The **Thames Path** can also be joined here (see page 66).

West of Oxford *p65*
Boating
Cotswold Boat Hire, The Trout Inn, St John's Bridge, Farringdon Rd, Lechlade on Thames, T01793-727083, same-day enquiries T07947-993784 (mob). Rowing boats, electric boats and day cruisers.

Riverside (Lechlade) Ltd, Park End Wharf, Lechlade, T01367-253599, www.riverside-lechlade.co.uk. For rowing boat, motor boat and cruiser hire.

⊖ Transport

Oxford *p57, map p58*
Bicycle
Oxford is great for cyclists. You can hire a bike for a day, week or month from **Walton St Cycles**, 78 Walton St, T01865-311610.

Bus
Local Most local buses, including services to **Witney**, **Minster Lovell** and **Burford**, are run by **Stagecoach Oxford**, T01865-772250.

Long distance The intercity and local bus terminus is at Gloucester Green, very close to the city centre. **National Express**, T08717-818178, www.nationalexpress.com, for **London Victoria** and long distance. Also the **Oxford Tube**, T01865-772250 (24-hr London–Oxford express service).

Car
Car hire Thrifty, Osney Mead, T01865-250252; **Oxford Hatchback Hire**, Longcot, Shotover Kilns, Old Rd,

Headington, T01865-763615; **Midlands Vehicle Rental Ltd**, www.mvrltd.co.uk.

Car parks Central car parks (many of which have hefty overnight charges) include Gloucester Green, Westgate, Worcester St, Abbey Pl and Oxpens Rd. Park and Ride is run by **Oxford Bus Co**, T01865-785400. Day return bus fare £1.50.

Taxi
Relatively cheap in Oxford, and it's not usually a problem finding one on the street. Otherwise **City Taxis** T01865-201201; 24-hr minicabs from **001 Taxis** T01865-240000.

Train
The main railway station is in the west of the city, where the Botley Rd meets Hythe Bridge St, a 15-min walk from the centre. Trains are run by First Great Western, T0845-700 0125, www.firstgreat western.co.uk, and Virgin Trains, T0871-9774222, www.virgintrains.co.uk.

West of Oxford *p65*
Taxi
A to B Taxis, Kerrieview, Burford Rd, Minster Lovell, T01993-706060; **Fairways Airport & Tour Cars**, Burford, T01993-823152.

❶ Directory

Oxford *p57, map p58*
Hospitals John Radcliffe Hospital, Headley Way, Headington, T01865-741166, is the nearest casualty department.

Worcestershire and Herefordshire

Worcestershire is most famous for its elegant and watery Malvern Hills, inspiration for no less a great cause than the *Enigma Variations*. And once you start exploring Worcester, it becomes clear that the town has a lot going for it, especially if superb bars, pubs, restaurants and some really stylish shopping opportunities are your thing.

Along with its northern neighbour Shropshire, Herefordshire still just about remains one of the least 'spoiled' counties in England. Famous for its ruddy cattle, it hardly deserves its bovine reputation. Hops, hedgerows and rural scenes are what the county does best. Anyone in search of villages, landscapes and locals who have yet to embrace the tourist dollar could do worse than start looking here. This well-wooded border county was never industrialized and agriculture has continued here on a smaller scale than elsewhere. Halfway up, the old market town of Ledbury and then the capital Hereford both reward visitors thanks to their unhurried way of life and outstanding local produce. To the west, just over the border in Wales, the town of Hay-on-Wye has become synonymous with the book trade. Tourist activity in the north of the county tends to stick to the Black and White village trail around the delightful town of Leominster.

Worcester, the Malverns and the Vale of Evesham → *For listings, see pages 85-90.*

Worcester is a perfect gem of a city nestling on the banks of the Severn river to the south of the Malvern Hills, some of the best countryside the West Midlands has to offer. The city is full of great history, quirky shops and beautiful medieval streets. Sir Edward Elgar, its most famous son, is commemorated admirably both in the Cathedral (a magnificent structure) and in the nearby countryside where he grew up and which was often the inspiration for his music. To the southeast, the town of Evesham is swaddled in delightful and highly productive countryside best-known for its market-gardening and spring blossom.

Arriving in Worcester, the Malverns and the Vale of Evesham

Getting there There are regular **First Great Western** trains ① *www.firstgreatwestern. co.uk*, from London Paddington to Shrub Hill Station Worcester, the journey takes around two hours 15 minutes. There are also regular **London Midland** trains ① *www. londonmidland.com*, from Birmingham New Street to Worcester Foregate Street, which is more convenient for the centre.

The M5 is an excellent nearby thoroughfare and by exiting at Junction 7 you'll get to Worcester very quickly. This serves travellers from Birmingham in the north and as far southwest as Exeter. Coming from London, the M4 joins the M5 just outside Bristol or if you prefer a more historical route passing through Oxford, you can take the M40 to Birmingham and then the M42 will connect you with the M5. **National Express** coaches ① *www.nationalexpress.com*, stop on the edge of the city at the Sixways Park and Ride, and links to scheduled city bus services.

The City stands on the banks of the River Severn and the Worcester & Birmingham Canal so there are plenty of opportunities to get a **boat** either from Bristol and Cardiff, or a canal barge from Birmingham.

Getting around Making your way round Worcester centre can be fraught with frustration because of one major two-lane road that divides most of the town from the wonderful Cathedral Precinct. Once you're away from this road, however, much of the centre is pedestrianized.

Information TIC ① *The Guildhall, High St, WR1 2EY, T01905-726311, www.visitworcester. com, Mon-Sat 0930-1700.*

Worcester

On a purely visual level, Worcester does have an extraordinary range of spectacular street architecture from imposing Georgian Churches converted into smart bars to perfect examples of early Tudor buildings which have been pubs for over 300 years. There's an old saying that Worcester has a different pub for every day of the year and it's true that Friar Street – the superlatively preserved mainly Elizabethan and Tudor pedestrianized walkway – is a cornucopia of great restaurants, pubs and even smarter shops than those on the High Street.

The Guildhall is as good a place as any to start your trip round Worcester and even though it's a walk from Foregate Station, you'll get a taste of how smart Worcester is. Designed by a local, Thomas White, the building looks like an 18th-century palace from the outside with its amazing wrought iron gate and Italianate façade. The real glories, however, are reserved for the inside and the **Assembly Room** ① *T01905-723471*, which is like a beautiful highly decorated ballroom, but now full of the worthy burghers of Worcester wolfing down roast dinners – the place is also a self-serve restaurant and tea room.

The Hive ① *Sawmill Walk, The Butts, WR1 3PB, www.thehiveworcester.org*, opened in July 2012 and is a joint university and public library. Beyond the striking interior, it also houses the collections that used to reside in the History Centre and offers genealogy and history buffs some fascinating resources. For those who want to learn more about Worcester in a more visual manner, the **Worcester Museum and Art Gallery** ① *Foregate St, WR1 1DT, T01905-25371, www.whub.org.uk, Mon-Sat 10930-1630, free*, can be found nearby.

Turning right from The Pheasant Inn, a three-storey Tudor building dating from 1540, you will be facing down Friar Street, in the direction of the main reasons for being there, namely the great historic sights, bijou shops and restaurants that typify this touristic paradise. **Greyfriars** ① *(NT) Friar St, WR1 2LZ, T01905-23571, www.nationaltrust.org.uk, see website for opening times, £4.60, child £2.30, family £11.50*, from which the street takes its name, is probably Friar Street's oldest building. Its imposing, somewhat forbidding, gabled rear-end runs down the side of Friar Street, but it's only accessible from a picturesque walkway running off on the left, a little way down from The Pheasant. Built as a townhouse in 1480 next to a very early medieval monastery, this site dates from the beginnings of the Cathedral in the 10th century. There's also a really magnificent walled garden.

From here it's a short walk to **The Tudor House** ① *Friar St, T01905-612309, www.tudorhouseworcester.org.uk, Wed and Sun 1000-1600 and Thu in summer, free*, which used to be the Museum of Local Life. The house is staffed entirely by volunteers and there are displays relating to Worcester's history, as well as the house and the Tudor period.

Once you do make it into the grounds of what has been called 'the most beautiful cathedral in Britain' you begin to realize what all the fuss is about. It's not as majestic as Salisbury, as weird as Exeter or as imposing as Durham but if you want a church where you can really feel the mystery of history and the awe people must have felt a thousand years ago when they saw the majesty of this holy place, then **Worcester Cathedral** ① *Chapter Office, 8 College Yard, WR1 2LA, T01905-732900, www.worcestercathedral.co.uk, 0730-1800, free, guided tours are available*, is for you. Not that the Cathedral was above burying the odd unholy man, such as King John whose body lies in a tomb near the main altar. In a codicil to his will he asked to be buried in Worcester Cathedral and being 'the faithful city', they obliged with a handsome tomb closer to the most sanctified part of the building than anyone else. Apart, that is, from **Prince Arthur's Chantry** which was built to house the remains of Henry VIII's elder brother. There's also a **Norman Crypt** – the oldest in the country – some really lovely Victorian stained glass which rivals Notre Dame and Canterbury, and an intriguing Georgian outbuilding called **The Guesten House** which is only be available for corporate events.

The Cathedral Precinct consists also of **The King's School** and the world-renowned **Choir School**. Every year the Cathedral Choirs of Worcester, Hereford and Gloucester get down and strut their funky stuff in competition with each other. **The Three Choirs Festival** (see page 89) takes place in Worcester once every three years.

Leaving the Cathedral square by **The Edgar Gate** which looks as if it could be the inspiration for Worcester's Coat of Arms you enter a little network of streets but have to cross the dreadful Sidbury road to get to **The Commandery** ① *Sidbury, WR1 2HU, T01905-361821, www.whub.org.uk, Mon-Sat 1000-1700, Sun 1330-1700, £5.50, child £2.50, family £13*, which started life around the time of St Wulfstan, founder of the current Cathedral in the 11th century. The place was originally a hospital where the sick were tended to by monks, but it really came into its own when a local wealthy clothier called Wylde put what was now his family home at the disposal of **Charles II** and his Royalist Army prior to the Battle of Worcester in 1651. It manages to score with a really thorough presentation on the history of this turbulent time, complete with a tableau of the sentencing of Charles I to death by beheading.

Just across the road from the Commandery, the **Worcester Porcelain Museum** ⓘ *Severn St, WR1 2ND, T01905-21247, www.worcesterporcelainmuseum.org.uk, Easter-31 Oct Mon-Sat 1000-1700, 1st Nov-Easter Tue-Sat 1030-1600*, is the perfect contrast to the blood, guts and diseases of the Commandery. This great little museum which shows you how the elite have coped with changing trends in place-settings over the last 300 years and there's a fabulous shop showcasing the work of the oldest continuous porcelain manufacturer in the country.

Around Worcester

There is a wonderful attraction a little way out of Worcester, the **Elgar Birthplace Museum and Visitor Centre** ⓘ *Crown East Lane, Lower Broadheath, WR2 6RH, T01905-333224, www.elgarmuseum.org, museum open daily 1100-1700, £7.50, child £3.50, family £15*. It is accessible by public transport, buses from Worcester Crowngate bus station run to nearby Crown East Church and less frequently past the museum (www. worcestershirebus.info), but easy to reach by car. Here you'll find all manner of Elgar treasures with regular concerts of his work and rare manuscripts to help you unlock the secret of the man who wrote 'Land of Hope and Glory', as well as a brilliant cello concerto. You'll also be in striking distance of the beautiful Malvern Hills (see below) where Elgar probably came up with that famous piece of patriotism.

There's one other place near Worcester that's really worth a visit if you're a fan of stately ruins and excellent sculpture – as well as the odd monster. **Witley Court and Gardens** ⓘ *(EH) Worcester Rd, Great Witley, WR6 6JT, T01299-896636, www.english-heritage.org.uk, see website for opening times, £6.50, child £3.90, family £16.90*, is maintained by English Heritage and is a really stunning and spooky ruin surrounded by some important work by 18th-century monumentalist sculptor Nesfield.

The Malvern Hills

For some, England has no more beautiful countryside to offer than the Malvern Hills, an ancient and mysterious eruption of 650-million-year-old granite and crystalline rock. Pushing their way upwards dramatically from the surrounding flat landscape, the hills lie a few miles southwest of Worcester and divide the counties of Herefordshire and Worcestershire. The aptly named 'Land of Hope and Glory' may well have been inspired by the composer Elgar's frequent visits to this extraordinary and serene geographical anomaly, and he certainly first conceived the original tune upon which the *Enigma Variations* were based while walking here. William Langland, a 14th-century Christian radical mystic, was also so moved by the incomparable countryside that he was struck by a vision which became the basis for the epic poem *Piers Plowman*.

Information TIC ⓘ *21 Church St, WR14 2AA, T01684-892289, www.visitthemalverns.org, daily 1000-1700 (Sun Nov-Mar 1000-1600)*.

Malvern

The logical place to start, whether you're a walking fan or a water fan attracted to the famous English rivers Severn, Avon and Teme, is really the town of Malvern, which actually consists of seven different 'Malverns' spread around the slopes of the hills, from **West Malvern** via **Great Malvern** to **Little Malvern** in the south. Great Malvern is really the centre, with fantastic views to the west over the town as well as being the best starting point for the obligatory walk on the hills. It's also the oldest part of Malvern and because of its remoteness was chosen by the Norman Benedictine Monks for the location of the Great Priory Church (see below), built in 1085. Malvern continued as a relatively sleepy location until the 19th century when ailing city types and sophisticates were drawn by the famous Malvern 'water-cure', now transformed into a thriving bottled spring water business. Consequently, this Victorian blooming led to the architectural flavour of much of the town, best exemplified by Bellevue Terrace, a sort of faux Georgian front which runs at right angles to Church Street, the main drag of Great Malvern.

The magnificent 11th-century **Priory Church** ① *Parish Office, Church St, WR14 2AY, T01684-561020, www.greatmalvernpriory.org.uk*, has a rich heritage going back over 900 years. The building itself is a combination of Norman and Perpendicular Gothic and has some extraordinary stained glass depicting a rare example of the *arma Christi* – the wounds of Christ – which miraculously survived the English Reformation. The **gatehouse** originally housed visitors to the Abbey, dates back to around 1400 and is an extraordinarily ornate structure which now is the location of **Malvern Museum** ① *The Priory Gatehouse, Abbey Rd, WR14 3ES, T01684-567811, Mar-Oct daily 1030-1700, £2, child 50p, Sun free*. There's a fascinating exhibit on the water-cure doctors and their hydropathic establishments, and the bottling of water since 1622.

The TIC will supply you with a plethora of walking guides to the Hills, but the best way to get to them is via the **North Hill** and **Worcesterhire Beacon**, at the north end of the range. The reward for reaching the top is a truly amazing view – one of the best in England and from which it is said you can see six counties. Luckily there's somewhere you can fortify yourself before attempting this climb: **St Ann's Well Café** ① *St Ann's Rd, WR14 4RF, T01684-560285, www.stannswell.co.uk*, reached from right next to the TIC via a leafy path and 99 steps. It's a lovely little building dating back to 1815, which became very popular for those taking the water-cure as there's a fresh-water spring on site. An elaborately carved font is one of the main attractions and you can still 'take the waters' here (although a highly conscientious note from the council suggests that you boil it first). For those not wishing to take a risk, there's a more recently built octagonal extension to St Ann's Well which houses a superb café with some wonderful cake.

Other unmissable treats of the region include **Upton-upon-Severn** which used to be an important port on the Severn and still houses a splendid marina as well as The **Upton Heritage Centre** ① *Church St, WR8 0HT, T01684-592679, spring and summer 1030-1630*, in an extraordinary building known as *The Pepperpot*. The **TIC** ① *Church St, WR8 0HT, T01684-594200, www.visitthemalverns.org*, is a good place to find out about local accommodation and events, the most famous of which is the Upton Jazz Festival which usually takes place during the last weekend of June.

The Vale of Evesham

Evesham owes its beginnings to a humble swineherd called Eoves who in AD 709 had a vision of the Virgin Mary while searching for an escaped pig in an area called 'The Lomme'. Unable to believe his eyes, he persuaded his boss, Ecgwin, Bishop of Worcester, to come and have a look. The bishop was so impressed by the quality of the vision and the general holiness of the location that he decided to build a great Abbey there, which at the height of its power was one of the top three most important religious sites in the country.

Easily reached from Birmingham on the A435 or from Oxford in the south on the A44, the area around Evesham produces most of the country's fruits and probably the best asparagus in the world (which is cheap, available in virtually every pub, restaurant and hotel and served, in the local style, with brown bread and plenty of delicious butter). The optimum time for experiencing what the local tourist Tsars have dubbed 'The Blossom Trail' is from mid March to mid May. The plum orchards explode with colour first, rapidly followed ten to 14 days later by the apple blossoms.

Evesham itself is a bustling market town with its roots going back to well before the Middle Ages. The River Avon has always played a central part in the history of the town and in the 19th century became the chief reason for it becoming so popular with Victorian day trippers who saw messing about on the water as a healthy, wholesome outdoor pursuit akin to cycling and walking. To this day there's a plethora of boating activities to be explored, and one of the best is the trip boat *Handsam Too* ① *www.handsamboatcompany.co.uk*, which can be boarded in Abbey Park, right next to the Almonry and **Tourist Information Centre** ① *Almonry Heritage Centre, Abbey Gate, WR11 4BG, T01386-446944, www.almonryevesham.org, Mon-Sat 1000-1700, Sun 1400-1700.* The **Almonry** is a wonderful and extremely well-preserved 14th-century building which also used to be the home of the chief Entertainments Officer of the Abbey. It now contains a museum spread out over a warren of period rooms which reflect the town's history. There's a particularly interesting exhibit on local lad Simon De Montfort, arguably the founder of Parliamentary Democracy.

Evesham Abbey was largely dismantled at the orders of Henry VIII in 1540, but the tourist people have thoughtfully provided markers as to the original structure's boundaries and still standing are the twin churches of All Saints and St Lawrence and Abbot Lichfield's fine 16th-century bell tower. These buildings within the Abbey precincts form an impressive backdrop to the **Abbey Park** with its grassy banks, shady trees and flower beds sweeping down to the River Avon (where some of the best boat trips and angling are to be had for miles around). The Battle of Evesham, the last skirmish of the Baron's War against an autocratic monarchy, was fought here in 1265. De Montfort led the charge for the Barons but was defeated by Edward, Henry III's son. His body was hacked to pieces and sent to the far flung corners of the Kingdom. However, the monks of the Abbey were able to save a fragment of De Montfort's remains and buried him with due ceremony before the High Altar of the Abbey, a spot now commemorated by a simple Stone Memorial.

Hereford and around → *For listings, see pages 85-90.*

Hereford has a slightly stodgy reputation which is really unfair. In fact, it's a dignified, solidly built place on the banks of the Wye in the process of reinventing itself as a 'City of Living Crafts' thanks to the growing reputation of its technical college. Craft shops and cottage industries are doing well here, part of an increasingly diversified rural economy. Approached from the east across the broad floodplain of the Lug, unmissable sights in the city include the diminutive cathedral and its most prized possession: the Mappa Mundi. This extraordinary survival from the Middle Ages, a parchment atlas of the world, is on display in a purpose-built annexe of the cathedral that also provides room for the largest chained library in the world (see page 82). The Cathedral also plays host to The Three Choirs Festival every three years, the oldest event of its type in Europe.

The countryside around Hereford repays a visit with its sleepy and smart little villages. The meanderings of the Wye run past rolling hills until they meet the Welsh border at Hay-on-Wye, second-hand book centre of the free world. To the north, the 'Black and White' village trail leads up through half-timbered settlements clustered around ancient churches towards charming old Leominster with its impressive Priory church, flourishing bric-a-brac shops and market produce.

Arriving in Hereford

Getting there There are a few direct **trains** a day from London Paddington to Ledbury, Hereford and Leominster (taking around two hours 40 minutes to three hours), but generally you will have to change either at Newport in Wales or Worcester. It's also at least a two-hour journey to the area from Birmingham via Worcester. Hereford is 20 miles west of Junction 2 of the M50, bypassing Ledbury on the A417 and the A438, about three hours' **drive** from London. **National Express** ⓘ *www.nationalexpress.com*, run five coaches a day to Hereford from London Victoria, taking about four hours.

Getting around Local **bus** services (patience needed to reach the outlying villages) are run by **First** ⓘ *www.firstgroup.com*. **Stagecoach** ⓘ *www.stagecoachbus.com*, head into South Wales. All the towns in the area are easily walked around.

Information Discover Herefordshire Centre ⓘ *1 King St, HR4 9BW, T01432-268430, www.visitherefordshire.co.uk, Mon-Sat 0930-1700, Sun 1000-1600*. **Ledbury TIC** ⓘ *38 The Homend, HR8 1BT, T01531-636147, www.visitledbury.info, Mon-Sat 1000-1700*. **Leominster TIC** ⓘ *1 Corn Sq, HR6 8LR, T01568-616460, www.leominstertourism.co.uk, Mon-Sat 0930-1600*. **Hay-on-Wye TIC** ⓘ *Oxford Rd, HR3 5DG, T01497-820144, www.hay-on-wye.co.uk, Oct-Dec 1100-1300 and 1400-1600, Dec-Feb 1100-1300*.

Hereford

Hereford is a solid, red-brick, Victorian-looking town on the banks of the river Wye, very much the heart of its county. The centre of the town today is **St Peter's Square**, a triangular road junction dominated by the imposing neoclassical Shire Hall. A few strides west lead into High Town past the Old House. Dating from 1621, the **Old House** is now a faintly forlorn-looking survival at one end of High Town, the broad pedestrianized open space in the middle of town lined with all the big brand names in retail. The ancient Jacobean half-timbered building contains a **museum** ⓘ *Old House Museum, High Town, HR1 2AA, T01432-260694, www.beta.herefordshire.gov.uk/museums, all year Tue-Sat 1000-1700, Apr-Sep: Sun* *and bank holiday Mon 1000-1600*, reconstructing a few period rooms. Look out especially for the bargeboard carving of a cow being tugged at from both ends by two farmers, a lawyer milking their argument in the middle.

South of St Peter's Square, **Castle Green** is an early Georgian prom overlooking Castle Pool, still very pretty and a delightful place to picnic near the river. The park was laid out on the site of the city's Norman castle, hence the name. From here Castle Street provides the most attractive approach to Hereford's idiosyncratic **Cathedral** ① *5 College Cloisters, Cathedral Close, HR1 2NG, T01432-374200, www.herefordcathedral.org, 0915-evensong (1730 or 1530 on Sun) daily for visitors*. Dedicated to St Ethelbert, it's an endearingly small-scale affair, much of its well-weathered knobbly old pink stone covered in green lichens, situated in an atmospheric little close just north of the river. The building demonstrates just about the entire gamut of English cathedral architecture: the great round pillars of the Nave with their carved capitals stepping the unexpectedly short distance down to the carved 14th-century choir; beyond the High Altar, the Lady Chapel is one of the finest examples of the 13th-century Early English style in the country; the tower and eastern transept are good examples of 14th-century Decorated. Other highlights of the interior include the early 16th-century Chantry of Bishop Audley and the Early English crypt, the most recent (13th century) of its kind in the country.

Next to the Cathedral, in a modern purpose-built cloister-style library building funded by Sir Paul Getty, the church's ancient **chained library** ① *Mappa Mundi and Chained Library, Apr-Nov Mon-Sat 1000-1700, Oct-March Mon-Sat 1000-1600, £6, concessions £5, family £14* (the largest of its type in the world), has been restored and reconstructed. It makes an appropriate setting for the extraordinary **Mappa Mundi**, a medieval world atlas that puts the Holy Land firmly at the centre of things. The Mediterranean Sea divided the known world into three parts: Asia, Europe and Africa. Britain is drawn much larger than it should be and is marked up with a variety of cathedral towns. Elsewhere there be dragons and depictions of various scenes from the Old Testament.

From the Cathedral Close, narrow Gwynne Street (named after Nell, the local actress who won the heart of Charles II) leads down to the **Left Bank Village** and the **Old Wye Bridge**. A pleasant stroll can be taken over the pedestrianized stone bridge to the **Bishop's Meadow** and across the Victoria Footbridge back into Castle Green. A right turn on Bridge Street heads back towards the middle of town and Broad Street, home to the **Hereford Museum and Art Gallery** ① *Broad St, T01432-260692, Tue-Fri 10-1700, Sat 1000-1700, Apr-Sep Sun and bank holidays 1000-1600, free*, and also the **City Library**. The small museum holds a variety of Roman artefacts found nearby at Kentchester, while the library has a particularly good selection of local history reference books. Broad Street, graced by the marvellous balconies of the **Green Dragon Hotel**, joins up with the High Street at the top end of High Town, where stands **All Saints' Church** with a slightly twisted spire, early 13th-century decoration in the nave and very good café ① *www.cafeatallsaints.co.uk*. Narrow medieval streets such as **Capuchin Lane** (also known as Church Street and Church Lane), lead back to the Cathedral from High Town.

Marooned in the north of the town, beyond the livestock market on Widemarsh Street, are the ruins of the **Blackfriars Monastery** ① *St John Medieval Museum and Coningsby Hospital, Widemarsh St, HR4 9HN, T01432-274903, Easter-Oct Wed-Sat 1100-1500*, with a museum that explains the site's link with the crusading Knights Templar and a chapel that is still used by the Order of St John. Worth seeking out on a rainy day is the **Hereford Cider Museum and King Offa Distillery** ① *Pomona Pl, HR4 0EF, T01432-354207, Apr-Oct Mon-Sat 1000-1700 (last admission 1615), Nov-Mar Mon-Sat 1100-1500 (last admission 1415), open Bank Holiday Sun, £5.50, concessions £5, child £3, family £16*. This former cider-making factory displays equipment and cider-making paraphernalia explaining how the journey from apple to glass.

West of Hereford to Hay-on-Wye

The Weir ① *(NT)*, Swainshill, HR4 7QF, T01981-590509, *www.nationaltrust.org.uk*, *see website for opening times*, £5.70, children £2.90, family £13.50, five miles west of Hereford on the A438, is a beautiful riverside garden designed by Repton, well worth a look in spring for its bluebells and snowdrops, with commanding views over the Wye and into the Black Mountains beyond.

Arthur's Stone ① *(EH)*, *www.english-heritage.org.uk*, *see website for opening times*, *free*, seven miles east of Hay-on-Wye off the B4348 near Dorstone is quite an impressive prehistoric burial chamber, its mound of earth stripped away to reveal the huge stones at its core. From Dorstone, the B4348 runs down the beautiful **Golden Valley** alongside the river Dore. Nestling in the green acres here, the remains of the Cistercian monastery at **Abbey Dore** ① *HR2 0AA*, *www.doreabbey.org.uk*, *Abbey open dawn to dusk, free*, are a remarkable survival, thanks in part to the attentions of the Scudamore family in the 17th century, who perhaps felt remorseful about their ill-gotten gains after the Dissolution. The nearby **Abbey Dore Court Gardens** ① *HR2 0AD*, *www.abbeydorecourt.co.uk*, *Mar-Sep Mon, Thu, Sat and Sun 1100-1700*, £4, is a must-see for garden lovers.

In the village of **Wormelow**, seven miles southwest of Hereford, a tiny **museum** ① *Cartref*, *Wormelow*, *T01981-540477*, *www.violette-szabo-museum.co.uk*, *Apr-Oct Wed 1100-1300 and 1400-1600, phone to check opening times, donation requested*, of old photographs and mementoes, commemorates Violette Szabo, the SOE (Special Operations Executive) agent who was parachuted several times into occupied France. She was eventually captured and executed shortly before the end of the war. The museum is in the house that used to belong to her cousins and where she used to rest up at between missions. The 1958 film *Carve Her Name with Pride* was inspired by her wartime activities.

About five miles from both Wormelow and Abbey Dore, **Kilpeck Church** is an extraordinary Norman survival, richly carved and reputed to be the finest example of its type in the country. The church's red sandstone has withstood the weather over the centuries, and the vivacity and sheer variety of the different carvings – a pig, wrestlers, rude women and dogs – is astonishing.

Back on the A438, just beyond Whitney, a little old **toll bridge** ① *www.whitneybridge. co.uk*, 80p, takes the B4350 over the Wye and past **Clifford Castle**, three miles north of Hay-on-Wye. This very overgrown and ruined medieval fortification is properly picturesque, unprettified and almost unvisited. An atmospheric and forlorn place beside the river.

Hay-on-Wye

Something of a phenomenon, over the last four decades Hay-on-Wye has been transformed into an international centre for second-hand books. Now it makes for a seriously enjoyable destination for anyone searching for illumination and fed up with mass-market retailing and dumbed-down attractions. Just over the border in Wales, surrounded by wooded hills and sheep-cropped fields, its wonderful position on the banks of the Wye would justify a visit in itself. Bookworms, though, will find themselves in seventh heaven. Steep narrow little streets are lined with shops laden with books ancient and modern. A clambering browse up to the small hilltop **castle** is bound to turn up a few irresistible surprises, although prices can be high too. The castle is now inhabited by the self-proclaimed King of Hay himself, local man Richard Booth. He was largely responsible for the town's renaissance, establishing his bookshop here in 1961 and never looking back. An ardent supporter of all things regional, local and decentralized, he has been helped in his crusade by the success of the annual **Literary Festival** in early June, founded here in 1988 by Norman Florence and his son Peter.

Crossing the Wye, still quite narrow here, from Hereford, a right run onto Broad Street leads into the town's main square below the town clock. From here almost all the bookshops are within easy walking distance, most of them on the way up to Castle Street and the TIC at the top of the town.

East of Hereford

Ledbury is a dignified market town nestling beneath the Malvern Hills, halfway between Hereford and Gloucester. Famous for its half-timbered Jacobean market hall at the top of the High Street, the place could make a good alternative base to Worcester for exploring the Malverns. Nearby is an immaculate Gothic Romantic folly built in 1812 by the Hervey Bathurst family, **Eastnor Castle** ⓘ *just outside Ledbury on the A449, HR8 1RL, T01531-633160, www.eastnorcastle.com, Easter-Sep check website for days and times*, designed by Robert Smirke. The family still live there in considerable splendour surrounded by a deer park, arboretum, lake and a truly unmissable interior stuffed with medieval tapestries and other delights such as the Pugin Room.

Hellens ⓘ *Much Marcle, HR8 2LY, T01531-660504, www.hellensmanor.com, Easter-Sep Wed, Thu, Sun and bank holiday Mon afternoons by guided tour at 1400, 1500, 1600, £7, child £4, family £15*, three miles south of Ledbury, is a strange old manor house first built in 1245 and almost continuously occupied by the same family down to the present day. A variety of unusual historical mementoes connected with the likes of Charles I, James II and Anne Boleyn are displayed amid ancient rooms with a vaguely contrived air of antiquity.

North of Hereford

Black and White village trail is the star attraction north of Hereford. This circular driving route will take you through some of the prettiest villages in England; **Weobley** is the quintessential example, with the **Red Lion** hotel nestling in a village of black timber-frame and white brick. **The Olde Salutation Inn** ⓘ *www.salutation-inn.com*, ensconced behind topiary hedges, could hardly be more typical of the area.

The town of **Leominster** can repay a visit thanks to its market square and quiet air of unhurried calm. School Lane is an alleyway of interesting independent shops, with the Merchant's House tearoom nearby. East of Leominster, rolling green hills stretch along the A44 to Bromyard.

Hampton Court Castle and Gardens ⓘ *Hope Under Dinmore, near Leominster, HR6 0PN, T01568-797777, www.hamptoncourt.org.uk, Mar-Nov daily 1030-1700*, one of the most important early fortified manor houses in England, has been transformed by garden designer Simon Dorrell. A little tower in the Maze reached by a secret tunnel is just one of its many surprises.

Just north of Leominster, **Berrington Hall** ⓘ *(NT) HR6 0DW, T01568-615721, www.nationaltrust.org.uk, see website for opening times*, is the home of an astonishing costume collection, which Colonel Wade used to surprise guests such as Graham Greene, Virginia Woolf, JB Priestley and John Betjeman at Snowshill Manor, his home in the Cotswolds. Only some costumes are on display at any given time but the collection can be viewed by appointment. Berrington Hall itself is an austere neoclassical pile overlooking Capability Brown-landscaped gardens and the Brecon Beacons, with a surprsingly delicate and elegant interior.

Wigmore Castle ⓘ *(EH), www.english-heritage.org.uk, see website for opening times, free*, eight miles west of Ludlow on the A4110, is a ruined medieval fortress that has subsided into itself over the centuries, leaving its curtain walls and towers surrounding a mess of crumbling masonry that kids love to scramble over.

Worcestershire and Hertfordshire listings

For hotel and restaurant price codes and other relevant information, see pages 9-12.

⊝ Where to stay

Worcester *p76*

£££ The Worcester Whitehouse Hotel, 62 Foregate St, Worcester, WR1 1EA, T01905-24308, www.worchesterhotel.co.uk. A comfortable billet right next to the hustle and bustle of Foregate and the station, and very convenient if you've arrived by train. Try and secure a quieter room at the back.

££ The Diglis House Hotel, Severn St, WR1 2NF, T01905-353518, www.diglis househotel.co.uk. The nicest thing about this hotel is its location nestling right on the river bank in a beautifully preserved old part of Worcester, and it's only a few mins' walk from the centre. Rooms could do with some refurbishment though.

££ Fownes Hotel, City Walls Rd, WR1 2AP, T01905-613151, www.fowneshotel worcester.co.uk. This converted glove factory is a little bit outside the city centre but is extremely tasteful, has an à la carte restaurant and is a really comfortable base from which to enjoy Worcester in style.

££ Pear Tree Inn and Country Hotel, Smite, Worcester WR3 8SY, T01905-756565, www.thepeartree.co.uk. About 15 mins' drive from the centre of Worcester, this hotel is popular for conferences and weddings. Rooms are clean and the food is good, and despite being very close to the M5 well soundproofed. Prices rise at weekends.

££ Premier Inn, Wainwright Way, Warndon, WR4 9FA, T0871-5279188, www.premierinn. com. Near the M5 and a few miles from the centre, this follows the usual **Premier Inn** pattern. There's a Beefeater next door.

££-£ Little Lightwood Farm, Lightwood La, Cotheridge, WR6 5LT, T01905-333236, www.lightwoodfarm.co.uk. About 3 miles from Worcester, the farm offers a 3-bed self-catering log cabin. Take the A44 out

of Worcester in the direction of Broadwas, after about 4 miles you'll find a turning to the right into Lightwood La (direction Lower Broadheath). The farm is about half a mile up the road. Min weekly stay.

Malvern *p79*

££ Ashbury Bed & Breakfast, Ashbury, Old Hollow, WR14 4NP, T01684-574225, www. ashburybedandbreakfast.co.uk. This small B&B is about 15 mins' walk from the town centre and a good starting point for walking the Malvern Hills. Clean, comfortable rooms and some excellent home cooking.

££ Bredon House Hotel, 34 Worcester Rd, WR14 4AA, T01684-566990, www. bredonhouse.co.uk. A fairly small but impeccably respectable establishment enjoying spectacular views from the vantage point of the main Worcester Rd and also very near to the middle of Great Malvern.

££ Como House, Como Rd, WR14 2TH, T01684-561486, www.comohouse.co.uk. A lovely 1850s' Malvern stone house this is a good value, comfortable hotel within easy walking distance of Malvern town centre. They're also most obliging about lifts to the station and good vantage points for walks.

Vale of Evesham *p80*

££££-£££ Wood Norton Hotel, Wood Norton, Evesham, WR11 4YB, T01386-420007, www.thewoodnorton.com. Definitely the poshest hotel in the region, this place used to be known as Wood Norton Hall. A beautiful grade II listed Victorian building nestling in 170 acres of glorious parkland undoubtedly the best place to experience The Vale in bloom.

££ Brookside Guesthouse, 11 Brookside, WR11 2ND, T01386-443116, www.brookside-guesthouse.com. Welcoming B&B, a short walk along the river to the town centre.

££ Northwick Hotel, Waterside, Evesham, WR11 1BT, T01386-40322, www.northwick hotel.com. A handsome Georgian building right next to the river and packed full of amenities. About 5 mins from Evesham station so is pretty handily situated both for the town and The Vale.

Hereford p81

££££-£££ Castle House, Castle St, Hereford, HR1 2NW, T01432-356321, www.castlehse. co.uk. In the most picturesque part of town and with beautifully appointed rooms.

£££ The Green Man, Fownhope, about 5 miles southeast of Hereford on the B4224, T01432-860243, HR1 4PE, www. thegreenman.co. Pretty gardens not far from the River Wye and plenty of historical associations stretching back centuries at this welcoming family-run hotel.

££ Green Dragon Hotel, Broad St, Hereford, HR4 9BG, T01432-272506, www.greendragon-hereford.co.uk. Genuinely ancient, refurbished **Heritage** hotel in the middle of the city, close to the cathedral, more impressive outside than in but unbeatably convenient.

Around Hereford p83

££££-£££ Feather's Hotel, 25 High St, Ledbury, HR8 1DS, T01531-635266, www.feathers-ledbury.co.uk. Characterful accommodation, some rooms with 4-poster beds. Has a spa and a popular restaurant.

£££ The Pandy Inn, Dorstone, HR3 6AN, T01981-550273, www.pandyinn.co.uk. The inn dates back to the 12th century and serves reasonable food (see below), the very pleasant rooms are in a modern timber construction.

£££ The Stagg Inn and Restaurant, Titley, HR5 3RL, T01544-230221, www.thestagg. co.uk. Has 3 en-suite bedrooms above a destination food pub in delightful border village about 12 miles west of Leominster (see page 87). Also the option to stay in the nearby Grade II-listed Vicarage.

££ The Old Rectory, High St, Pembridge, T01544-387968, HR6 9EU, www.theoldrectory pembridge.co.uk. A beautiful B&B with welcoming and helpful hosts. Recommended.

Hay-on-Wye p83

NB Book early if you plan to stay during the Hay Festival.

£££ The Swan at Hay, Church St, HR3 5DQ, T01497-821188, www.swanathay.co.uk. A Georgian mansion in the middle of town, very clean and with a well-maintained with a garden. Good food served in the restaurant.

£££-££ Kilverts Inn, The Bullring, HR3 5AG, T01497-821042, www.kilverts.co.uk. Rooms named after famous authors, relaxed and informal atmosphere. The bar is popular with locals and can be noisy.

£££-££ Seven Stars B&B, 11 Broad St, HR3 5DB, T01497-820886, www.theseven-stars. co.uk. Bang in the middle of things, with an indoor heated pool and comfy rooms.

£££-££ Tinto House, 13 Broad St, HR3 5DB, T01497-821556, www.tinto-house.co.uk. A Georgian townhouse, built around 1780, opposite the Clock Tower. Has a homely feel with the owner's paintings hung around the place.

££ The Bear Bed & Breakfast, 2 Bear St, HR3 5AN, T01497-821302, www.thebearhay. com. A very stylish B&B with a warm welcome and spotless rooms.

££ Belmont House, Belmont Rd, HR3 5DA, T01497-820718, belmonthouse9@ btinternet.com. An antiquey B&B with large bedrooms, at the bottom of Castle St.

££ The Start, HR3 5RS, T01497-821391, www.the-start.net. An 18th-century house a short walk from the centre of town, down by the river, with a large garden. Great hosts.

££ York House, Hardwicke Rd, Cusop, HR3 5QX, near Hay-on-Wye, T01497-820705, www.york-house.eu. An elegant, late Victorian residence on the edge of Hay-on-Wye, also with large, southerly facing gardens and aiming for a country house atmosphere. Min 2 nights at weekends.

££-£ Old Black Lion, Lion St, HR3 5AD, T01497-820841, www.oldblacklion.co.uk. Comfortable rooms and highly rated food.

Camping

£ Radnors End, Hay-on-Wye, a short walk over the river, HR3 5RS, T01497-820780, www.hay-on-wye.co.uk/radnorsend. A campsite with all the facilities you'd expect, and there's also an apartment to rent on a weekly basis.

❷ Restaurants

Worcester p76

££ Bindles, Church St, WR1 2HU, T01905-611120, www.bindles.co.uk. Tucked away behind Church St, this place has attractive decor and the food's pretty good, too.

££ Bombay Palace, 38 The Tything, Worcester, WR1 1JL, T01905-613969. A deservedly popular Indian restaurant.

££ Carluccio's, Chapel Walk, Crowngate Shopping Centre, WR1 3LD, T01905-612040, www.carluccios.com. **Carluccio's** has come to Worcester. Open all day, with pasta, meat dishes and good hot chocolate.

££ Four Seasons, 61 Lowesmoor, WR1 2RS, T01905-27026, www.fourseasonsrestaurant. co.uk. As good a Chinese as you'll find in this town, with friendly helpful waiters.

££ Pasha Indian Cuisine, 56 St John's, WR2 5AJ, T01905-426327, www.pasha-online.co.uk. An innovative approach to the food of the subcontinent.

££-£ Little Venice, 1-3 St Nicholas St, WR1 1UW, T01905-726126, www.littlevenice. uk.com. A simple, modern trattoria that resembles **Pizza Express**, but it's a good family place and reasonable value for money.

Hereford p81

There's not yet a huge variety of choice in the town.

££-£ Thai on Wye, 15 West St, HR4 0BX, T01432-376769, www.thaionwyerestaurant. co.uk. Good value and delicious Thai food.

£ Café in All Saints' Church, High St, HR4 9AA, T01432-370415, www.cafeatallsaints. co.uk. From hot specials such as burgers or casserole to sandwiches and cake. A good stop for breakfast, lunch or afternoon tea inside the church.

£ Rocket Café, 43 St Owen St, HR1 2JB, T01432-271234, www.rocketcafe.biz. A charming café offering quiches, soups, sandwiches and cakes, as well as a wonderful range of salads made with seasonal and organic ingredients.

Around Hereford p83

£££-££ Crown and Anchor, Cotts Lane, Lugwardine, HR1 4AB, a couple of miles east of Hereford on the road to Ledbury, T01432-851303, www.crown-anchor.co.uk. Another beamed pub but with an accomplished menu. Prides itself on the selection of whiskies on offer. Restaurant and bar menu available.

£££-££ The Stagg Inn and Restaurant, Titley, HR5 3RL, T01544-230221, www.the stagg.co.uk. A destination food pub with accommodation –see page 86) and food that has attracted the attentions of the Michelin inspectors.

££ Carpenter's Arms, Walterstone, HR2 0DX, T01873-890353, www.thecarpenters armswalterstone.com. A cosy cottage pub close to the Welsh border and the Black Mountains with reasonable pub grub.

££ The Pandy, Dorstone, T01981-550273, www.pandyinn.co.uk. A dinky old free house (apparently the oldest in Herefordshire) with a reasonable but limited menu. In the wonderful Golden Valley east of Hay. See also Where to stay, page 86.

££ Ye Olde Salutation Inn, Weobley, HR4 8SJ, T01544-318443, www.salutation-inn.com. A superb village local in an ancient black and white building with a smartish restaurant attached.

££-£ The Bell, Bosbury, 4 miles north of Ledbury off the B4214, HR8 1PX, T01531-640285, www.thebellatbosbury.com. Has bar skittles, and is another ancient black and white pub in an interesting little village where the tower got separated from its church. Serves pies, pizzas and pub grub.

£ Grape Vaults, 4 Broad St, Leominster, HR6 8BS, T01568-611404, www.thegrape vaults.co.uk. A snug, cosy and creaky little town pub serving pub grub. About the 8 miles from Hereford but north of the A465.

£ Ye Olde Steppes, Pembridge Village Shop & Tearoom, High St, HR6 9DS, T01544-388506, www.yeoldesteppes. co.uk. A traditional tearoom, settle yourself in the parlour and you'll be hard pressed to leave. A selection of loose-leaf teas, home-made cakes, sandwiches and daily specials. The attached shop sells some great local produce as well as sweets and some essentials. Recommended.

Hay-on-Wye p83

In addition to the listings below, the **Old Black Lion** and **The Swan at Hay**, see Where to stay above, serve good food.

£££-££ The Three Tuns, Broad St, HR3 5DB, T01497-821855, www.three-tuns.com. Damaged extensively by fire some years back, this is now a very nice gastropub offering traditional and international dishes, as well as a good wine list.

££ The Granary Café and Restaurant, Broad St, T01497-820790. At the top of the approach from Hereford is a wholesome vegetarian as well as cottage pie type place with waitress service.

££ Red Indigo, 10 Castle St, HR3 5DF, T01497-821999, www.redindigo.co.uk. Good Indian restaurant with friendly staff.

££-£ Blue Boar, Castle St, HR3 5DF, T01497-820884. Popular and does good pub food.

🍷 Pubs, bars and clubs

Worcester p76

The Courtyard, 11 St Nicholas St, WR1 1UW, T01905-23050, www.courtyardworcester pub.co.uk. This place is riotous at weekends with some good music events in an extremely historic setting. It's worth a visit if you like your evenings hot and sweaty.

Farriers Arms, 9 Fish St, T01905-27569. Another historic location with extremely well-kept beer and a very homely atmosphere.

Horn and Trumpet, 12 Angel St, WR1 3QT, T01905-29593, www.horntrumpetworcester. co.uk. Very popular with the locals, this place isn't your typical inner city pub.

The Pheasant Inn, 25 New St, WR1 2DP, T01905-729 862, www.pheasantworcester. co.uk. Probably the oldest building you'll ever have a drink in, this is a stunning 15th-century structure which used to be famous for cock-fighting but is now home to a sports bar.

Swan with Two Nicks, 28 New St, WR1 2DP, T01905-28190, www.theswanwithtwonicks. co.uk. Extremely picturesque, hosts live music.

Malvern p79

Farmers Arms, Birts St, Birtsmorton, Malvern, WR13 6AP, T01684-833308, www.farmersarmsbirtsmorton.co.uk. A bit sleepier than some of the other Malvern pubs, it nevertheless is worth a visit for its cosy ambience and family atmosphere.

Vale of Evesham p80

The Fleece, The Cross, Bretforton, near Evesham, WR11 7JE, T01386-831 173, www. thefleeceinn.co.uk. This place is a definite must for fans of ale and history. It's a 15th-century National Trust property, kept in its original condition with three open fires and beamed ceilings. Among the delights it offers are a large orchard to drink in, B&B rooms and good pub grub. Really idyllic.

🎭 Entertainment

Worcester p76
Music

Huntingdon Hall, Crowngate, WR1 3LD, T01905-611427, www.worcesterlive.co.uk. A splendid building, complete with organ and stained glass, it also has live music, comedy and spoken word events.

Keystones Café Bar, 1 Copenhagen St, WR1 2HB, T01905-731437, www.keystones cafebar.co.uk. If you prefer your music a bit more modern, this is an excellent bar and restaurant underneath the street and even

has a fragment of 13th-century archway on the dance-floor. Live music every Sat.
Worcester Cathedral, 8 College Yard, WR1 2LA, T01905-732900, www.worcester cathedral.co.uk. Some of the best music in the country can be heard here, and not just from the choir. It's an outstanding acoustic and orchestral works played here will have never sounded better.

Theatre
Worcester Swan Theatre, The Moors, WR1 3ED, T01905-611427, www.worcesterlive. co.uk. A charming city theatre, putting on the usual diet of thrillers, musicals and pantos, but a reasonably professional company if you like that sort of thing.

❀ Festivals

Worcester *p76*
Aug The **Three Choirs Festival** (mid-Aug), The Guesten, 15 College Green, WR1 2LH, T01905-616200, www.3choirs.org. Probably one of the most prestigious musical festivals in the world and even though Worcester shares it with Hereford and Gloucester, it's definitely worth catching it. Tickets can be purchased online.
Nov-Dec Worcester City Christmas Fayre. An extremely successful Victorian themed street market which takes place every year and attracts thousands. Stallholders get all dressed up in Victorian costume and there's plenty to distract the kids.

Malvern *p79*
Jun Upton Jazz Festival, www.uptonjazz. co.uk. A weekend of Jazz at the end of Jun, complete with camping.

Vale of Evesham *p80*
Apr-Jun British Asparagus Festival, www.britishasparagusfestival.org. A host of asparagus themed events over the course of 8 weeks, including the AsparaBus and AsparaFest.

Hay-on-Wye *p83*
May-Jun Hay-on-Wye annual literary festival, www.hayfestival.com.

🛍 Shopping

Worcester *p76*
In **Mealcheapen Street** you'll find F Durrant and Son, www.fdurrantandson.com, a stockist of country and sporting stuff, including shotguns. The proprietor will give you advice about huntin', shootin' and fishin' in the area. Just round the corner you'll come to **Reindeer Court** a superb covered market featuring some very special places such as **The Worcester Antiques Centre**, T01905-610680, which is an Aladin's cave of affordable and not so affordable antiques from every period. Nearby is one of Worcester's smartest modern jewellers **Rock Lobster**, 21 Reindeer Court, www. rocklobsterjewellery.com, which looks minimal on the outside, but the prices certainly aren't.
Finally, whatever you do, don't forget the shopping opportunities afforded by **Worcester Porcelain Museum** (see page 78).

Around Hereford *p83*
The Old Chapel Gallery, East St, Pembridge, HR6 9HB, T01544-388842, www.oldchapel gallery.co.uk. Displays an eclectic range of handicrafts and artworks by local artists and craftsfolk, and has an upstairs gallery given over to temporary exhibitions. Open daily.

Hay-on-Wye *p83*
Books
Addyman Books, 36 Lion St, HR3 5AA, T01497-821136, www.hay-on-wyebooks. com. Specialist in modern 1st editions and English literature.
C. Arden Bookseller, The Flat, Cranbourne Hse, The Pavement, HR3 5BU, T01497-820471, www.ardenbooks.co.uk. Natural history books, there is no longer a shop and most sales are completed online but

if you're in Hay and want to have a look at their stock give them a ring.

Hay Book Company, Grove House, High Town, HR3 5AE, T01497-821641, www.haybooks.com. A great place to search for old and out of print books.

Hay Cinema Bookshop, Castle St, T01497-820071, HR3 5DF, www.hay cinemabookshop.co.uk. A huge and rambling shop in an old cinema, with a bewildering range of books on offer.

Hay-on-Wye Booksellers, 13/14 High Town, HR3 5AE, T01497-820875, www.hayonwye booksellers.com. Good general stock of second-hand books and new books at reduced prices.

Mostly Maps, 2 Castle St, HR3 5DF, T01497-820539, www.mostlymaps.com. For antique maps and prints.

Murder and Mayhem, 5 Lion St, HR3 5AA, T01497-821613. Owned by the same people as Addyman Books (see above), this is the place to come for detective fiction, true crime and horror.

Richard Booth's bookshop, 44 Lion St, HR3 5AA, T01497-820322, www.booth books.co.uk. Has a fine blue frontage in the middle of Hay with tiles outside depicting domesticated livestock and a mustachioed man, apparently not a caricature of the King himself.

⏱ What to do

Worcester *p76*
Cricket
Worcestershire County Cricket Club, New Rd, WR2 4QQ, T01905-337921, www.wccc.co.uk.

Fishing
Bransford Game Fishery and Fisherman's Lodge, Hill End Farm, Station Rd, Bransford, WR6 5JJ, T01905-830548.

Quad biking
Peachley Quad Trekking, Peachley La, Lower Broadheath WR2 6QR (Sat Nav WR2 6QX), T01905-641309, www.peachleyquadtrekking.co.uk.

Racing
Worcester Racecourse, Pitchcroft Grandstand Rd, WR1 3EJ, T01905-25364, www.worcester-racecourse.co.uk.

Tennis
Cripple Gate Park Tennis Courts, Cripplegate Park New Rd, WR2 4QG, mnewell@worcester.gov.uk.

Hereford *p81*
Boating
Kingfisher Cruises, 44 Ethelstan Crescent, HR2 7HR, T01432-267862, www.wyenot. com. Mar-Oct, for 45-min riverboat trips on the Wye.

Walking
Guided Walks of Hereford by **Guild of Guides**, T01432-356270, www.hereford guidedwalks.org.uk. £3, May-Sep, departing Visit Herefordshire Centre Mon-Sat 1100 and Sun 1430. Haunting and Horror Walk on Wed from Jul-Sep 1915.

ⓘ Directory

Worcester *p76*
Hospitals Worcestershire Royal Hospital, Charles Hastings Way, WR5 1DD, T01905-763333. **Library** The Hive, Sawmill Walk, The Butts, WR1 3PB, T01905-822866, www. thehiveworcester.org. **St John's Library**, Glebe Close, St. John's, WR2 5AX, T01905-822722. **Police** Castle St, WR1 3QX, T101. **Post office** 8-10 Foregate St, T0845-7223344.

Shropshire

Shropshire remains one of England's proud-to-be-undiscovered corners. Like Herefordshire, its relatively low population density and tenacity to traditional farming have resulted in one of the least spoiled of England's rural landscapes. Shrewsbury is its county town, variously pronounced 'Shrozebury' or 'Shroosbury', a well-to-do castellated market town in a lovely position on the River Severn. A string of very attractive little towns runs south parallel to the border with Wales on the A49 south of Shrewsbury: Church Stretton for hillwalkers and Ludlow for antique collectors and gourmands, to name a couple. The Severn Valley from Shrewsbury embraces the unassuming delights of Much Wenlock and then the well-packaged tourist attractions at Ironbridge, 'birthplace of the Industrial Revolution'. Quiet old towns, hillwalking, nature reserves and industrial heritage are the county's forte as far as visitors are concerned. In fact whatever Shropshire does, whether it's food, farming or family fun, it does it well, beautifully backward and happily isolated from the rest of the UK.

Shrewsbury and around → *For listings, see pages 97-99.*

The county town of Shropshire, Shrewsbury makes up for the lack of a medieval cathedral with a variety of smaller examples of ecclesiastical architecture, quite an impressive old castle and a picturesque situation. Almost an island in a loop of the Severn river, this market town has been a fortified site since at least the fifth century. Visitors arriving by train still have to make their way beneath the castle walls up into the centre. Ignored by the Luftwaffe in the Second World War, many of the Tudor half-timbered buildings still survive. One of the best examples, Rowley's House, is currently an excellent local history museum full of remarkable Roman finds (it will be relocating at the end of 2013 to the Music Hall). Other sights worth seeking out include three remarkable churches – St Mary's, the ancient Abbey of the Holy Cross, and St Chad's. It's the unhurried pace and quiet atmosphere of this famously unpronounceable place that make it such a good base for exploring one of England's most lovely lost corners.

Arriving in Shrewsbury

Getting there There are hourly **trains** from London Euston, changing either at Crewe or Birmingham, taking around 2½ to three hours depending on the connection. Shrewsbury is also linked by **rail** to the north and Birmingham.

Shrewsbury is most easily reached from the south on the M54 from Junction 11 on the M6. It's about three hours 30 minutes from London. For details on parking, refer to

Shrewsbury

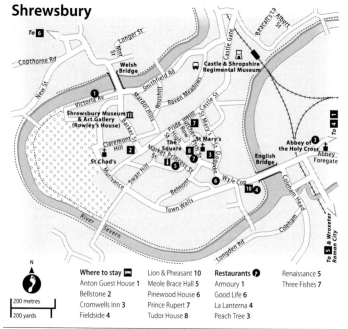

N

200 metres
200 yards

Where to stay 🛏
Anton Guest House 1
Bellstone 2
Cromwells Inn 3
Fieldside 4

Lion & Pheasant 10
Meole Brace Hall 5
Pinewood House 6
Prince Rupert 7
Tudor House 8

Restaurants 🍴
Armoury 1
Good Life 6
La Lanterna 4
Peach Tree 3

Renaissance 5
Three Fishes 7

Walks in Shropshire

See www.shropshirewalking.co.uk for additional information on routes and to download walking leaflets.

The Long Mynd: four miles there and back. Start: Church Stretton. A fairly steep climb up rocky paths to the top of Shropshire's great ridge overlooking Wales. OS Map: Explorer 217, Landranger 137.

The Stiperstones: four miles there and back. Start: The Bog, six miles north of Bishop's Castle. A walk up to the eerie Devil's Chair with views into Wales and Shropshire. OS Map: Explorer 216, Landranger 137.

Downton: five mile circle. Start: Downton on the Rock, seven miles by road west of Ludlow. Riverside walks along the Teme and woodland paths past the ruins of Victorian industry. OS Map: Explorer 203, Landranger 148.

The Wrekin: two miles there and back. Start: Little Wenlock, six miles north of Much Wenlock. Popular climb up a volcanic plug for distant views of Shrewsbury and the Severn. OS Map Explorer 242, Landranger 127.

Titterstone Clee Hill: two miles there and back. Start: Bitterley, three miles east of Ludlow. A short climb up to a superb viewpoint overlooking Ludlow in the distance. OS Map: Explorer 203, Landranger 137.

www.visit shrewsburytourism.com. Regular **National Express** ⓘ *www.nationalexpress.com*, services run from London, Birmingham and elsewhere, arriving at the **bus** station a few hundred yards from the **train** station.

Getting around The town itself is easily negotiated on **foot**. The surrounding countryside really needs a **car**, although a network of local buses to places such as Much Wenlock are run by **Arriva**, www.arrivabus.co.uk, and several other companies. The **Travel Shropshire** website ⓘ *www.travelshropshire.co.uk*, is a good planning tool.

Information Shrewsbury TIC ⓘ *Rowleys House Museum, Barker St, SY1 1QH, T01743-281200, www.visitshrewsbury.com, Oct-Apr Mon-Sat 1000-1700, May-Sept Mon-Sat 1000-1700, Sun 1000-1600.* At the end of 2013, the TIC will be moving back to its original home in the Music Hall.

Places in Shrewsbury

From the station, a few steps away the steep **Castle Gate** heads up into the heart of the town. The Castle itself dates largely from the 14th century, with a few 18th-century alterations, and contains the **Shropshire Regimental Museum** ⓘ *Castle St, SY1 2AT, T01743-358516, www.shropshireregimentalmuseum.co.uk, Easter-mid Sep Fri-Wed 1030-1700, Sep-mid Dec and Feb-Easter Mon-Wed, Fri-Sat 1030-1600 but times are variable so ring in advance, £2.50, concessions £1.50.* One of the largest of its kind in the country, the museum contains the usual collection of military memorabilia, weapons, uniforms, china and medals, but on an impressive scale, while the Norman motte is worth climbing for views over the town.

A couple of hundred yards beyond the castle, off Castle Street on the left, the soaring 200-ft spire of **St Mary's Church** ⓘ *SY1 1EF, Apr-early Dec Mon-Sat 1000-1700, early Dec-Mar Mon-Sat 1000-1600,* dominates the old part of town. The closest the town comes to a cathedral, set in a pretty little close, the church displays a satisfying mix of Norman and Gothic architectural styles and contains a remarkable Tree of Jesse in the beautiful east window, imported from old St Chad's. Much of the other glass is also very fine, including a variety of French medieval craftsmanship.

Next on the left a few yards up Pride Hill, the continuation of Castle Street, **Butcher Row** is a particularly well-preserved street of half-timbered Tudor houses, with the **Abbot's House** on the corner of Fish Street an especially grand example. Two more – **Owen's Mansion** and **Ireland's Mansion** – can be seen a little further up Pride Hill where it joins the High Street leading into the Square, the centre of town and the late Geogian Music Hall. The Old Market Hall here is also Elizabethan.

A hundred yards north of the Square, down Barker Street, the **Shrewsbury Museum & Art Gallery** ① *T01743-258885, www.shrewsburymuseums.com, Mon-Sat 1000-1700, May-Sep also Sun 1000-1600, free,* in Rowley's House is well worth seeking out. Originally a warehouse for wool, built in the late Elizabethan era, the next door building was the first in the town to be made of brick. As well as many Roman finds from Wroxeter (see below) – including a mirror and the inscription over the town gate – and a medieval section, there's a highly rated Art Gallery with regular temporary exhibitions on local themes. The museum will be relocating in late 2013, however, to the Music Hall (see above). A similar distance west of the Square, up Claremont Hill, **St Chad's** is a very fine Georgian round church in a spectacular position overlooking the river with a prominent spire and elegant neoclassical portico. Apparently the building of it caused riots in protest at the demolition of part of the old town walls. Beyond the church, a spacious public park slopes down to the riverbank. From St Chad's, a charming walk down Murivance and Town Walls circles the town following the course of the river downstream to **English Bridge**, a venerable old stone structure and good viewpoint. Over the bridge, a hundred yards up Abbey Foregate, the **Abbey of the Holy Cross** ① *SY2 6BS, T01743-232723, www.shrewsburyabbey.com, Apr-Oct daily 1000-1600 (last entry 1545), Nov-Mar 1030-1500 (last entry 1445),* is a masterful Victorian improvement on a Norman foundation. Founded in 1083, the Abbey survived the dissolution thanks to its use by the laity as their local place of worship. Its greatest claim to fame these days is as the real-life home of Ellis Peter's fictional 'Brother Cadfael'.

Wroxeter

An interesting day trip can be made to **Wroxeter Roman City** ① *(EH), SY5 6PH, T01743-761330, www.english-heritage.org.uk, end Mar-early Nov daily 1000-1700, early Nov-late Mar Sat-Sun 1000-1600, £5.20, child £3.10, family £13.50.* On the evidence still standing today, 'City' seems a bit of an exaggeration, but five miles southeast of Shrewsbury, there are some fairly impressive remains of a place called Viroconium that once housed some 6000 souls, the fourth largest town in Roman Britain and part of Emperor Hadrian's fortification of his empire. The site of the baths and a large dividing wall can be seen, as well as a small museum of finds, although the best are in Rowley's House (see above).

There's also a working **vineyard** ① *Wroxeter, SY5 6PQ, T01743-761888, www.wroxeter vineyard.co.uk,* here which you can look round.

Church Stretton, Long Mynd and Wenlock Edge

South of Shrewsbury, the best walking country in Shropshire can be found around the small Victorian resort town of Church Stretton, easily reached on the train. The Long Mynd is a seven-mile ridge of rounded hills just to the west of Church Stretton. Lonely walks lead up to heights of 1700 ft through bracken, heather and gorse, the most famous of which is the **Burway**. The **Port Way** runs along the top of the ridge, providing fantastic views into Wales and inland England almost as far as Birmingham. Deep secret valleys run down the Long Mynd's eastern slopes, accessible from villages such as Little Stretton, Minton Batch and Priors Holt. Worth seeking out are the 20 or so acres of mixed deciduous woodland at **Old Rectory Wood**, just outside Church Stretton to the west. Details of all walks are available from Church Stretton **tourist information** ⓘ *T01694-723133, www.churchstretton.co.uk, Easter-Oct.*

Six miles west of the Long Mynd, the **Stiperstones** are another belt of high land, very different in character. Much of the area surrounding the Devil's Chair, a strange rock formation on the summit with ghoulish associations, is a National Nature Reserve. The Romans mined lead in these hills, an industry that thrived until the mid-19th century. White calcite waste tips from the mines can still be seen near **Snailbeach**. One old shaft has been preserved near **The Bog**, a village to the east of the Stiperstones themselves.

East of Church Stretton, **Wenlock Edge** is a long limestone escarpment running northeast from Craven Arms to Much Wenlock, overlooking Ape Dale to the west towards the Long Mynd. Halfway along it stands **Wilderhope Manor** ⓘ *(NT), Longville, near Much Wenlock, TF13 6EG, T01694-771363, www.nationaltrust.org.uk, see website for opening hours, £3.60, child £1.60, family £8.80,* an Elizabethan manor house in a beautiful position on the Edge, with wide views and scope for lovely walks in the surrounding woods. As it's a YHA hostel there may be limited access to some rooms.

At the northern end, **Much Wenlock** is a gem of a town with a very helpful **TIC** ⓘ *The Museum, High St, TF13 6HR, T01952-727679, www.muchwenlockguide.info,* and friendly locals. Narrow streets clamber away from the fine timbered Guildhall and the one main street. Nearby, the 12th-century Priory Ruins contain rare carvings and some well-kept topiary in the gardens.

Two miles east of the town, **Benthall Hall** ⓘ *(NT), TF12 5RX, T01952-882159, www.nationaltrust.org.uk, see website for opening hours, Feb £4.00, child £2.00, family £10.00, whole property £6.20, child £3.15, family £15.55,* at Broseley is a delightful 16th-century stone built manor house on the edge of the Severn Gorge. Still the home of the Benthall family, the interior features an impressive carved-oak staircase and elaborate plasterwork. Carefully tended old gardens lead down to a venerable little church dating back to the Restoration.

At the southern end of Wenlock Edge, near Craven Arms, **Stokesay Castle** ⓘ *(EH), SY7 9AH, T01588-672544, www.english-heritage.org.uk, see website for opening hours, £6.20, child £3.70, family £16.10,* is one of the best-preserved 13th-century fortified manor houses in the country. The timber-framed Jacobean gatehouse is worth a look in itself, giving onto a grassy courtyard and the little old castle. Built in the 1280s by one of the richest wool merchants in the country, Lawrence of Ludlow, the whole place has been beautifully restored by English Heritage and occupies an idyllic position in the valley. The most remarkable survival is the Great Hall with its arched timber roof and an ornate carved-wood Elizabethan fireplace in the solar or great chamber.

About eight miles west of Craven Arms towards the Welsh border, **Bishop's Castle** is a little border town and once the tiniest borough in England. Its Georgian town hall reflects this status, the dinky centrepiece of a town that could almost be a caricature of olde worlde charm, with its crooked-angled half-timbered buildings, ancient brewery and rolling hills all around.

Severn Gorge and Ironbridge

East of Much Wenlock, the **Severn Gorge** plunges down from a glut of ten museums at the **World Heritage Site** at **Ironbridge** (www.ironbridge.org) to the gorge-side town of

Bridgnorth. In Ironbridge, the first iron bridge in the world is still well worth a look after all these years. The result of three generations' worth of the Darby family's expertise in iron-smelting, it was erected in 1779. Now a well-preserved footbridge crossing the steep-sided gorge from the Victorian high street of the town, it forms the centrepiece of a pretty comprehensive celebration of the Industrial Revolution in Britain. An exhibition on the history of the bridge is housed in the original Tollhouse on the south side, over the bridge from the main drag of Ironbridge itself. The **Museum of the Gorge** ⓘ *TF8 7DQ, T01952-433424, www.ironbridge.org.uk, daily 1000-1700, passport tickets to all 10 museums, £24, child £15.25, family £65,* a short walk west on the north bank, traces the history of the whole gorge in an 1830s' warehouse, a highlight being the 40-ft scale model of the landscape in 1796. Up the road north from here in **Coalbrookdale** is the **Museum of Iron**, on the site of Abraham Darby I's original blast furnace of 1709, with which he succeeded in smelting iron with coke rather than charcoal. Also in Coalbrookdale are the **Darby Houses** and **Enginuity**, an Interactive Technology Centre where visitors are encouraged to try out the principles of engineering for themselves. Beyond Ironbridge is the **Jackfield Tile Museum** ⓘ *TF8 7LJ, T01952-433424, www.ironbridge.org.uk, daily 1000-1700,* a factory that was once a world centre for the decorative tile industry. Today, a huge collection of tiles from the Victorian era are on display. The nearby **Coalport China Museum** is housed in restored kiln workings, and don't forget to visit the **Tar Tunnel**, where a source of natural bitumen was discovered some 200 years ago.

In Bridgnorth, perched high above the river, you can ride up the 111-ft sandstone cliffs on the steepest funicular in the world, the **Bridgnorth Cliff Funicular Railway** ⓘ *6A Castle Terr, High Town & Underhill St, Low Town, WV16 4AH, T01746-762052 (station), www.bridgnorthcliffrailway.co.uk, Apr-Oct Mon-Sat 0800-2000, Sun 1200-2000, Nov-Mar Mon-Sat 0800-1830, Sun 1200-1830.*

Ludlow

The jewel in Shropshire's crown, Ludlow is a very picturesque hill town perched on the banks of the River Teme. Heavily fortified by the Normans under Roger Montgomery, the castle is still the main event, although just wandering around the town is also a joy. Ludlow **tourist information** ⓘ *Castle St, SY8 1AS, T01584-875053, www.ludlow.org.uk, Mon-Sat 1000-1700, also Apr-Oct Sun 1030-1700.*

Ludlow castle ⓘ *Castle Sq, SY8 1AY, T01584-873355, www.ludlowcastle.com, see website for opening hours, £5, child £2.50, family £13.50,* was slighted by Parliamentarians during the Civil War, but not as badly as many others. The superb views from the top of the Norman keep, the Great Hall, where Milton's *Comus* was first performed, and an unusual round royal chapel are some of the highlights of a visit. The castle has a long and troubled history at the centre of centuries of border clashes. Eventually it became the HQ of the Marcher barons, the seat of the Council of Marches established in 1475 to govern Wales. Many unfortunate Princes of Wales were associated with the place, including Arthur, elder brother of Henry VIII – married aged 14 to Catherine of Aragon but dead in his bed here soon after – and Edward, briefly Edward V before being deposed and possibly murdered by his uncle Richard III. The place is haunted by Marion de la Bruere, who inadvertently let enemies in through the gates with her lover. She stabbed him with his own sword and then threw herself from the Pendower Tower. Regular events are now staged within the castle walls, the best during the Ludlow festival in June and July.

A few hundred yards from the fateful castle gates, across Castle Square (scene of lively markets most days of the week), the neoclassical **Butter Cross** is the centre of town. Behind it, the **Church of St Lawrence** well deserves its status as 'Cathedral of the Marches'.

Evidence of the prosperity brought to the town by the wool trade, it contains a wealth of wonderful medieval glass, ancient tombs and royal misericords.

From the Butter Cross, **Broad Street** slopes down to the river, surely one of the most delightful streetscapes in the country. Before reaching the river at Ludford Bridge, with its lovely views of the river, it passes through the **Broad Gate**, the sole survivor of the town's seven medieval gates.

Shropshire listings

For hotel and restaurant price codes and other relevant information, see pages 9-12.

🛏 Where to stay

Shrewsbury and around *p92, map p92*
£££ Prince Rupert, Butcher Row, SY1 1UQ, T01743-499955, www.prince-rupert-hotel. co.uk. A smart hotel in the centre of town, in a cunningly refurbished old house on the corner of Butcher Row and Pride Hill.
£££ Tudor House, 2 Fish St, SY1 1UR, T01743-351735, www.tudorhouse shrewsbury.co.uk. A good and central B&B.
£££-££ Brompton Farmhouse B&B, Cross Houses, 4 miles south of Shrewsbury, SY5 6LE, T01743-761629, www.brompton farmhouse.co.uk. A highly rated B&B in a Grade II listed building.
£££-££ Cromwells Inn, 11 Dogpole, T01743-361440, www.cromwellsinn.co.uk. Opposite the Guildhall, atmospheric rooms above a wine bar.
£££-££ Lion and Pheasant, 49-50 Wyle Cop, SY1 1XJ, T01743-770345, www.lion andpheasant.co.uk. Comfortable, central hotel that serves good food.
££ Anton Guest House, 1 Canon St, SY2 5HG, T01743-359275, www.anton house.com. A very reasonably priced and friendly B&B not far from the centre.
££ The Bellstone, Bellstone, Shrewsbury, T01743-242100. Good value budget hotel in the centre of town with a brasserie attached.
££ Burlton Inn, Burlton, SY4 5TB, T01939-270284, www.burltoninn.com. On the road to Ellesmere, most people come here for the food. There are also some good rooms in an annexe behind the main building.

££ Fieldside, 38 London Rd, SY2 6NX, T01743-353143, www.fieldsideguesthouse. co.uk. Further out, but very comfortable.
££ Meole Brace Hall, Meole Brace, Shrewsbury, SY3 9HF (Sat Nav YS3 9JS), T01743-235566, www.meolebracehall.co.uk. Grade II listed house about a 20-min walk from the centre.
££ Pinewood House, Shelton Park, The Mount, SY3 8BL, T01743-364200, www.pinewoodbandbshrewsbury.com. A mile or so northwest of town, a 20-min walk, a B&B in a converted Victorian coach house that also offers a family flat. Recommended.
££ Soulton Hall, near Wem (Sat Nav SY4 5RS), T01939-232786, www.soultonhall. co.uk. Grand Elizabethan house with a family atmosphere, rooms in the main house and the Carriage House, and there's a 4-poster bed in the Cedar Lodge at the side of the walled garden. Also cottages to rent and fine dining. Recommended.

Church Stretton, Long Mynd and Wenlock Edge *p94*
££ Highlands B&B, Hazler Rd, Church Stretton, SY6 7AF, T01694-723737, www.highlandsbandb.co.uk. One of the better guesthouses in Church Stretton (which has more than enough to go round), with rooms overlooking the garden and views across the Long Mynd. Stays of 2 nights of more.
££ Old Brick Guesthouse, 7 Church St, Bishop's Castle, SY9 5AA, T01588-638471, www.oldbrick.co.uk. Friendly and central B&B with 5 rooms, very near a number of pubs. 2 night min stay at weekends.

££ Old Quarry Cottage B&B, Brockton, Much Wenlock, TF13 6JR, T01746-785596, www.oldquarrycottage.co.uk. 2 B&B rooms in the main house and the adjacent Coach House suite has its own kitchenette. Welcoming, with good walking nearby and tasty breakfasts.

££ Wenlock Edge Inn, Hill Top, near Much Wenlock, TF13 6DJ, T01746-785678, www.wenlockedgeinn.co.uk. Superbly positioned pub with acclaimed grub and comfortable rooms.

££-£ All Stretton Bunkhouse YHA, Meadow Green, Batch Valley, All Stretton, SY6 6JW, T01694-722593, www.yha.org. uk/hostel/all-stretton-bunkhouse. Ideal for walkers, bikers and birdwatchers.

£ The Talbot Inn, High St, Much Wenlock, TF13 6AA, T01952-727077. Fine pub grub in a beamed and welcoming village-style pub, which also has rooms in the converted Malthouse.

£ Willowfield Country Guesthouse, Lower Wood, All Stretton, near Church Stretton, SY6 6LF, T01694-751471, www. willowfieldguesthouse.co.uk. A peaceful, dignified place with attractive gardens.

£ YHA Wilderhope Manor, Longville in the Dale, TF13 6EG, T0845-371 9149, www. yha.org.uk/hostel/wilderhope. Recently refurbished hostel in the National Trust's Elizabethan manor house on Wenlock Edge (see page 95). Dorms and private rooms.

Ironbridge *p95*
£ Ironbridge Coalport YHA, High St, Coalport, TF8 7HT, T0845-371 9325, www.yha.org.uk/hostel/ironbridge-coalport. In a former china works building, boasts 80 beds in rooms and dorms.

Ludlow *p96*
££££ Mr Underhill's at Dinham Weir, Dinham Bridge, SY8 1EH, T01584-874431, www.mr-underhills.co.uk. A charming restaurant with swanky (if expensive) rooms on the river, a Michelin star for the food and a short bracing walk up into town.

££££-£££ Dinham Hall, Dinham, SY8 1EJ, T01584-876464, www.dinhamhall.co.uk. A grand 18th-century hotel beneath the castle walls with a good reputation for its food.

££££-£££ Overton Grange, Old Hereford Rd, near Ludlow, SY8 4AD, T01584-873500, www.overtongrangehotel.com. Another top-end option, a bit stuffy but also with an ambitious and accomplished menu, a short distance out of town towards Hereford on the B4361.

££ The Charlton Arms, Ludford Bridge, SY8 1PJ, T01584-872813, www.thecharltonarms. co.uk. Recently refurbished, overlooking the Teme rapids, close to the old town bridge.

££ Church Inn, The Buttercross, SY8 1AW, T01584-872174, www.thechurchinn.com. A cheerful freehouse, tucked away behind the Buttermarket bang in the middle of town, which has reasonable rooms and does very filling meals in a congenial atmosphere.

££ The Wheatsheaf Inn, Lower Broad St, SY8 1PQ, T01584-872980, www.the-wheatsheaf-inn.co.uk. At the bottom of Broad St, a pub with 5 clean, comfortable rooms.

££-£ Number Twenty Eight, 28 Lower Broad St, SY8 1PQ, T01584-875466, T0800-081 5000, www.no28ludlow.co.uk. A 16th-century townhouse below the Broad Gate, close to the river. A distinctly superior B&B.

🍴 Restaurants

Shrewsbury *p92, map p92*
£££-££ Renaissance, 29a Princess St, SY1 1LW, T01743-354289, www.renaissance restaurant.co.uk. Occupies grand Georgian dining rooms and uses seasonal fresh local produce. 6 Course Surprise Taster Menu on Fri and Sat evenings.

££ The Armoury, Victoria Quay, Victoria Av, SY1 1HH, T01743-340525, www.brunning andprice.co.uk/armoury/. Does modern British food in a converted warehouse restaurant-bar overlooking the river.

££ Good Life, 73c Wyle Cop, SY1 1XA, T01743-350455. Vegans and those looking for tasty gluten free options will love this place, but anyone will find something good to eat. If you have dietary restrictions and you're bored of polenta cake, the **Good Life** should make you smile.

££ The Peach Tree, 18-21 Abbey Foregate, SY2 6AE, T01743-355055, www.thepeach tree.co.uk. Tasty contemporary dishes served in a busy dining room. Does a 2 course for £10 evening special.

££-£ La Lanterna, St Julians, St Alkmunds Sq, SY1 1UH, T01743-233552, www.la-lanterna.co.uk. A popular old-school Italian trattoria.

££-£ The Riverside Inn, Cound, SY5 6AF, T01952-510900, www.theriversideinn.net. Does rooms (**££**) and some good British food on an attractive stretch of the river Severn.

££-£ Three Fishes, Fish St, SY1 1UR, T01743-344793. Worth seeking out for its excellent real ales in a fine Tudor building in the middle of town, as well as reasonably priced bar meals.

Church Stretton, Long Mynd and Wenlock Edge *p94*

££ Feather's Inn, Brockton, Much Wenlock, TF13 6JR, T01746-785202, www.feathersatbrockton.co.uk. A small menu but ingredients are fresh and local and the end result delicious.

££ Royal Oak, Cardington, near Church Stretton, SY6 7JZ, T01694-771266, www. at-the-oak.com. Tables outside and filling meals for lunch and dinner, close to Cardingmill Valley (NT).

££ Three Tuns, Salop St, Bishop's Castle, SY9 5BW, T01588-638797. Very old pub with its own brewery (granted a licence in the mid 17th century) serving pub grub.

Ludlow *p96*

£££ La Bécasse, 17 Corve St, SY8 1DA, T01584-872325, www.labecasse.co.uk. On the site of Hibiscus, which has since moved to London. A fine dining restaurant

that serves up dishes made from locally sourced produce. Set lunch menus (**££**) are good value.

£££-££ Koo, 127 Old St, SY8 1NU, T01584-878462, www.koo-ook.co.uk. Popular Japanese restaurant with à la carte and set menus.

££ Chiang Thai, 3 Market St, SY8 1BP, T01584-874212, www.thailudlow.co.uk. Above average Thai food down a narrow alleyway.

££ Roebuck Inn, Brimfield, 4 miles south of Ludlow, SY8 4NE, T01584-711827, www.theroebuckludlow.co.uk. Has a good reputation for its food.

££-£ Aragon's Restaurant, 5 Church St, SY8 1AP, T01584-873282. A café-restaurant that does filling sandwiches, soups, pastas and pizzas all day.

££-£ The Unicorn, 66 Corve St, T01584-873555, SY8 1DU, T01584 873 555, www. unicorn-ludlow.co.uk. Does above-average pub food in a cosy, beamed old place.

£ Ludlow Castle Tea Room, Ludlow Castle, SY8 1AY, T01584-878796, www.ludlow castle-restaurant.com. You don't have to visit the castle to eat here. A good lunch option with sandwiches, jacket potatoes and some delicious cakes and scones on offer.

For pub grub, see also **The Charlton Arms**, **Church Inn** and **The Wheatsheaf Inn** in Where to stay, above.

✿ Festivals

There are a number of local festivals, here are just a couple to consider:
Mar Shrewsbury Folk Festival, www. shrewsburyfolkfestival.co.uk. UK and World folk performers, as well as some dancing.
Jun Ludlow Arts Festival, www.ludlowarts festival.co.uk. Takes over the castle with theatre performances, music events in the town and an atmopshere of good-natured bonhommie.

Staffordshire

East of Shropshire and west of Derbyshire, Staffordshire is a Midland through-county that suffers by comparison. It lacks the landscape and the historical associations that draw people to its immediate neighbours. Even so, Stoke-on-Trent can boast some world-class industrial heritage and an optimistic forward-looking attitude. The city is in fact six separate towns – Tunstall, Burslem, Hanley (the city centre), Stoke, Fenton and Longton – and is consequently known as 'The Potteries'. These places were powerhouses of the Industrial Revolution, producing most of the famous chinas of the Victorian era on a mass scale using secret Chinese recipes. Some 15 miles south down the M6 sits Stafford, the county town but not a place many choose to linger over very long. They're more likely to head for the cathedral town of Lichfield, another 20 miles or so southeast across Cannock Chase, or to the UK's most popular theme park at Alton Towers, 15 miles east of Stoke-on-Trent.

Arriving in Staffordshire

Getting there

With **Virgin Trains** ① *www.virgintrains.co.uk*, and **London Midland** ① *www.london midland.com*, you can be assured of trains every 30 minutes for most of the day. **Cross Country Trains** ① *www.crosscountrytrains.co.uk*, run a local service from Birmingham and the West Midlands on a very regular basis. Handily situated just off the M6, Stoke-on-Trent is more or less slap bang in the middle of the country, so is easily accessible by **road** from all directions. From London take the M1 to Leicester and then the A50 takes you right into Stoke. Also the M40 from London will take you to Birmingham and you can get onto the M6 via the M42 and M5. Just after Newcastle-under-Lyme you turn right on to the A50 approaching Stoke from the west. From the southwest the M5 connects with the M6 outside Birmingham. From the north the M6 or the A1 will connect with the A50 for a fairly trouble-free journey.

Getting around

With plenty of parking and a far from pedestrianized centre Stoke-on-Trent and its surroundings are ideal for those with **cars**. The centre of the city is Hanley, even though there's also an area called Stoke. The town museum is situated in this area, though there are visitors' centres and factory shops attached to most of the functioning Pottery concerns. Stoke-on-Trent does, however, benefit from having an excellent **bus** service. **First** ① *www.firstgroup.com*, have a FirstDay ticket, priced £5 for an adult and £10 for a family (two adults and three children), which you can buy on any of their buses, and is valid for one day's unlimited travel on the local **First Network**.

Information

Stoke-on-Trent TIC ① *Victoria Hall, Cultural Quarter, ST1 3AD, T01782-236000, www.visitstoke.co.uk, Tue-Sat 1000-1600*. Comprehensive, helpful and conveniently situated. **Stafford TIC** ① *Gatehouse Theatre, Eastgate St, ST16 2LQ, T01785-619619, www.enjoystaffordshire.com, Mon-Fri 0930-1700, Sat 0900-1600*.

The Potteries → *For listings, see page 103.*

As their name suggests, the Potteries – aka Stoke-on-Trent – are best known for being a world centre of ceramics, home to such luminaries as Royal Doulton, Spode and Wedgwood. These businesses still dominate the daily life of Stoke-on-Trent, the city of six towns. Dickens described it as 'opulent', Arnold Bennett immortalized it as 'Knype' in his 'Five Towns' books such as *Clayhanger* and more recently Robbie Williams and Anthea Turner both spent their early lives imbibing the rich cultural mix and still flourishing nightlife of the city, which no doubt helped at least one of them on their way to international stardom. The manufacture of pottery in this area goes back to Roman times, but it wasn't until the coming of the Trent–Mersey Canal and the development of local coal-fields in the 18th and early 19th centuries that the place really took off, with the names listed above as well as quite a few others setting up factories which were soon generating handsome profits. An early exemplar of the truism 'where there's muck, there's brass', Stoke paid the price for this prosperity with legendary levels of pollution and some of the worst working conditions to be found in the country – a fact commemorated in one of the contemporary museums by a special 'child labour exhibit'. These days the urban landscape isn't quite so grimy and the famous bottle-kilns associated with Stoke – many of which are still standing – don't belch filthy smoke 24/7. Meanwhile kids aren't pressed into labour before they reach their teens, but are more likely to be found pressing their parents into taking them to Alton Towers, the nation's favourite theme park, which lies a few miles east of Stoke.

Most visitors to Stoke-on-Trent will want to head straight for its 'cultural quarter' and **The Potteries Museum and Art Gallery** ① *Bethesda St, ST1 3DW, T01782-232323, www.stokemuseums.org.uk, Mon-Sat 1000-1700, Sun 1400-1700, free.* Pick of the bunch, museum-wise, it is home to the largest collection of pottery in the world, as well as an original Spitfire fighter plane from the Second World War, which was designed by local lad Reginald Mitchell. Commemorating local lads of a different industrial background, there's also the **Coal Sculpture** which is a memorial to the two local colliers who died on picket duty during the 1984 miner's strike.

While there's an excellent narrative of the town's association with pottery in the town museum, an even better one can be found in the **Gladstone Pottery Museum** ① *Uttoxeter Rd, Longton, ST3 1PQ, T01782-237777, www.stokemuseums.org.uk, Apr-Sep daily 1000-1700, Oct-Mar daily 1000-1600, £7.25, child £5, concessions £5.75, family £21,* which is the only authentic reproduction of a Victorian pottery factory in the world and comes complete with cobbled yard and bottle-shaped oven-kilns. There's also a tearoom and gift shop.

For lovers of industrial history the **Etruria Industrial Museum** ① *Lower Bedford St, Etruria, ST4 7AF, T01782-233144, www.stokemuseums.org.uk, car park is on Kiln Down Rd, off Etruria Vale Rd,* is Britain's sole surviving steam-powered potter's mill. Built in 1857 to grind materials for the pottery industry it is open for events throughout the year (check the website for details) and offers a superb insight into how it all worked back in the days when there were many others like it.

Around Stoke-on-Trent → For listings, see page 103.

Seven miles north of Stoke-on-Trent, **Biddulph Grange** ① *(NT), Biddulph, ST8 7SD, T01782-517999, www.nationaltrust.org.uk, see website for opening times, £7, child £3.50, family £17.54,* is a Victorian fantasy garden. It features a variety of different 'rooms' in different styles from around the world, planted appropriately to their provenance. Highlights include the Egyptian Court, imitation Great Wall of China and the rockeries.

Visit the **Wedgwood Visitor Centre** ① *Wedgwood, Barlaston, ST12 9ER, T01782-282986, www.wedgwoodvisitorcentre.com, Mon-Fri 1000-1700, Sat and Sun 1000-1600, £10, concession £8, family £32, factory tour: Mar-Oct Mon-Thu, £2.50,* where there's a museum charting the history of Wedgewood the man and the pottery, crafts people at work, and a tour of the factory and an opportunity to see what it takes to call a cup a Wedgwood. There's also a shop and factory outlet, as well as a restaurant.

Some 20 miles east of Stoke-on-Trent, **Alton Towers** ① *Alton, ST10 4DB, T0871-222 3330, www.altontowers.com, daily from 16 Mar-10 Nov, daily 0930-2000 or dusk if earlier,* is the UK's most famous theme park. Thrill rides galore, including Nemesis and Oblivion, as well as river rapids, log flumes and Ice Age 4D to name but a few.

Near Stafford, the county town that has suffered thanks to the M6, the **Shugborough Estate** ① *Milford, ST17 0XB, T01889-881388, www.shugborough.org.uk, Mar-Oct mansion Wed-Mon 1100-1700 (last admission 1600), mansion open 1100-1300 for guided tours by our expert guides only, £15, child £9, family £37.50, gardens only £3.50,* is the 900-acre ancestral home of Lord Lichfield. Nearby, the **National Forest** ⓘ *www.nationalforest.org*, is a 200-square mile forest that impinges on three counties, with lovely woodland and walks.

Stafford is an undistinguished market town closely associated with Sir Izaak Walton, the *Compleat Angler*. Its main attraction is the Ancient High House, the tallest timber framed townhouse in England. Built in 1595 and refurbished with Elizabethan period rooms.

South of Stafford, **Lichfield** is an 18th-century looking market town with a surprisingly grand sandstone cathedral with three spires but little else to recommend it except a rather staid atmosphere. Its most famous inhabitant was Dr Johnson, the 18th-century man of letters, who was born and educated here, although he spent most of his life in London, passing through in later life on his way to Wales with his patrons the Thrales. Erasmus Darwin, Charles Darwin's grandfather, also lived here.

Staffordshire listings

For hotel and restaurant price codes and other relevant information, see pages 9-12.

⊖ Where to stay

The Potteries *p101*
£££ The Swan Hotel, 46-46a Greengate St, Stafford, ST16 2JA, T01785-258142, www.theswanstafford.co.uk. A good central option, this hotel has a decent restaurant (see below) and comfortable rooms, some with 4-poster beds.
££ Cathedral Lodge Hotel, Beacon St, Lichfield, WS13 7AR, T01543-414500, www.cathedrallodgehotel.com. 5-min walk uphill from the cathedral, a small (24 beds) family-run hotel that was once a sweet shop.
££ Express Holiday Inn, Stanley Matthews Way, Trentham Lakes, Stoke-on-Trent, ST4 4EG, T01782-377 000, www.express stoke.co.uk. Does a reasonable chain job.
££ Manor House, near Denstone, Uttoxeter, ST14 5DD, T01889-590415, www.4posteraccom.com. 3 miles away from Alton Towers is this ancient Tudor manor house B&B, very welcoming with double rooms with 4-poster beds and a self-catering cottage.

££ Slab Bridge Cottage, Little Onn Rd, Church Eaton, ST20 0AY, T01785-840220. A Victorian cottage on the Shropshire Union Canal, with 2 bedrooms with en suite bathroom and offering boat trips too.

⍦ Restaurants

The Potteries *p101*
££ Swan Brasserie, Swan Hotel, 46-46a Greengate St, Stafford, ST16 2JA, T01785-258142 www.theswanstafford.co.uk. Range of dishes from pasta to steak to Sri Lankan curry, and a decent wine list.
££-£ The Olive Tree, off the High St, 34 Tamworth St, Lichfield, WS13 6JJ, T01543-263363, www.lichfieldolivetree.co.uk. Does a Mediterranean menu in a buzzy and friendly atmosphere, there are Chef's specials and/or the 2- or 3-course Express Menu.
££-£ The Soup Kitchen, 2 Church Lane, Stafford, ST16 2AW, T01785-254775, www. thesoupkitchen.co.uk. This atmospheric and friendly place is a popular spot for lunch or afternoon tea and cake. The roof garden is open in fine weather.

Nottinghamshire and Derbyshire

Nottinghamshire is a through-county where the North meets the South and few visitors are likely to want to stop for very long with much more enticing places all around. The city of Nottingham itself is easily the main draw, an up-and-coming focus for nightlife and entertainment in the East Midlands, with a venerable history to match. Unfortunately, there really is precious little to recommend a special journey elsewhere in the county. Sherwood Forest is pushed hard by the Tourist Board, but is just a few hundred acres of waymarked paths through woods, the like of which can be found in more magical shapes and sizes all over the country. One place worth seeking out, though, is Newstead Abbey, the childhood home of Lord Byron and still strangely evocative of his peculiar strain of romanticism, admirably maintained by the County Council.

Some 15 miles west of Nottingham, Derby is usually seen as that city's poor relation. In fact it's a very different kind of place, making up for its lack of cool with some solid industrial heritage, mild-mannered local pride, very fine beer and an endearing cathedral. In the region are some fine old halls, houses and castles, well worth visiting.

Nottingham → *For listings, see pages 113-116.*

Like Newcastle, Nottingham has reinvented itself in recent years, this once-drab Midlands manufacturing centre now boasts Paul Smith designerwear, Nottingham Forest Football Club and a thriving nightlife and music scene. Once synonymous with hosiery and lace only bits of the old industrial city survive, much of it thankfully submerged beneath gloomy but marginally more liveable in housing projects and road junctions of the 60s. These bits are still likely to be of most interest to the visitor though: the area around the Lace Market and St Mary's church, neighbouring Hockley, and Nottingham castle, about two days' worth of exploration.

Arriving in Nottingham

Getting there East Midlands airport ① *www.eastmidlandsairport.com*, and **Birmingham International airport** ① *www.birminghamairport.co.uk*, are, respectively, 20 and 30 minutes away by car. There are regular **trains** from London St Pancras. Nottingham is 122 miles, or about two hours, from London by car, straight up the M1, one hour 30 minutes from Leeds further up the M1. At Junction 24, the A42 becomes the M42 on its way to Birmingham, about 30 minutes away. **National Express** ① *www.nationalexpress.com*, offers services throughout the country from Broadmarsh Bus Station, just south of the city centre. ▶▶ *See Transport, page 116, for more details.*

Getting around The centre of Nottingham, within a busy ring **road**, is easily small enough to negotiate on **foot**.

Information Nottingham City Information Centre ① *Smithy Row, off Market Sq, NG1 2BY, T08444-775678, www.experiencenottinghamshire.com, daily Mon-Sat 0930-1730, Sun 1100-1700.*

History

Unlike many Midland towns, Nottingham dates back to the Dark Ages. The Saxons settled in the area, only to be ousted by the Danes. When Edward the Elder took the town back in the 10th century, he built a bridge over the River Trent nearby and by the time the Normans arrived, Nottingham was the strategic key to the centre of the country. All that remains of the formidable stronghold they constructed is the gatehouse, much restored. The rest of the castle was demolished by the Parliamentarians after the Civil War. Shortly afterwards, the Duke of Newcastle built an Italianate mansion on the site, which was put to the torch itself during rioting over the Reform Acts in the 1830s. By that time, Nottingham was already a heaving industrial centre, riddled with slums, turning out hosiery and lace in huge quantities thanks to Hargreaves' Spinning Jenny and other technical breakthroughs. The Luddites smashed up the looms here with exceptional ferocity.

The city suffered considerable bomb damage during the Second World War, but it was only in the late 60s that Nottingham's traditional industries, including shoemaking, began to die on their feet. What looked like terminal decline has fairly recently been arrested with some bold enterprise initiatives, an injection of European cash, and by the never-say-die spirit of Notties themselves.

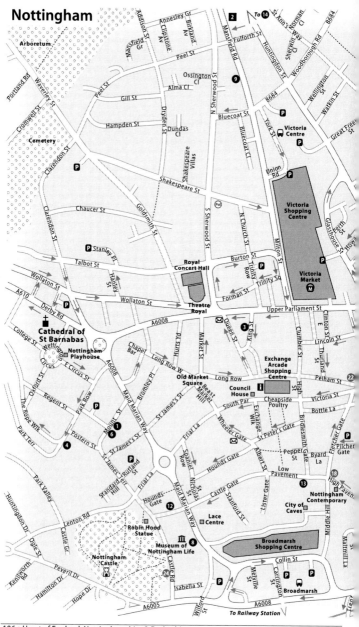

Nottingham

Arboretum

Annesley Gr

Addison St
Markfield Gr
Clipstone Av
Birkland Av

To 14

Peel St

Fulforth St

Mansfield Rd

St Ann's Norman

Sherwin Way

Woodborough Rd

B684

Portland Rd
Waverley St

Peel St

Ossington Cl
Alma Cl

N Sherwood St

Huntingdon St

Wellington St
Watkin St

Great Freeman St

Gill St

Dryden St

Bluecoat St

B684

York St

Victoria Centre

Hampden St

Dundas Cl

Bluecoat Cl

Cemetery

Clarendon St

Shakespeare Villas

Shakespeare St

Union Rd

Glasshouse St

Victoria Shopping Centre

Chaucer St

Goldsmith St

S Sherwood St

N Church St

Milton St

Pol

Clarendon St

Stanley Pl
Talbot St

Hanley St

Royal Concert Hall

Burton St
Trinity Row
Trinity Sq

Victoria Market

Wollaton St
A610
Derby Rd

Wollaton St

Theatre Royal

Forman St

Upper Parliament St

Clinton St E
Clumber St
Lincoln St
Thurland St
Howe

Cathedral of St Barnabas

A6008

Queen St

College St
Wellington Circus

Nottingham Playhouse

E Circus St

Chapel Bar

Long Row W

King St

Market St

Exchange Arcade Shopping Centre

High St

Pelham St

Victoria St

Bottle La

The Rope Wlk

Regent St

Park Row

Bromley Pl

Old Market Square

Long Row

Council House

Cheapside
Poultry

Exchange Wlk

St Peter's Gate

Park Ter

Mount St

Postern St

St James's St

Beast Market Hill
South Par

Friar La

Spaniel Row

Wheeler Gate

Albert St

Pepper St

Bridlesmith Gate

St Peter's Gate

Byard La
Pilcher Gate

Park Valley

The Ropewalk

Regent St

St James's Ter
Rutland St

Standard Hill

Friar La

Maid Marian Way

St Nicholas St

Hounds Gate

Castle Gate

Low Pavement

Lister Gate

Nottingham Contemporary

Fletcher Gate

High Pavement

Maid Marian Way

Huntingdon Dr
Castle Gr
Ogle Dr

Park Valley

Standard Hill

Lenton Rd

Hounds Gate

Robin Hood Statue

Nottingham Castle

Peveril Dr

Museum of Nottingham Life

Castle Rd

Lace Centre

Stanford St

City of Caves

Broadmarsh Shopping Centre

Middle Hill

St Mary's Gate

Maltmill La

Kenilworth Rd
Hamilton Dr
Hope Dr

Isabella St

Willoughby St

Collin St

Meville St

Carrington St

Broadmarsh

A6005

A6008

To Railway Station

N

100 metres

100 yards

Where to stay 🛏
Igloo Backpackers
  Hostel **2**
Lace Market **3**
Langar Hall **4**
Mercure **1**
Walton's **5**

Restaurants 🍴
4550 Miles from Delhi **1**
Emilio's **14**
French Living **3**
Hart's **4**
Jamie's Italian **13**
Laguna Tandoori **6**
Mem Saab **8**
Royal Thai **9**
World Service **12**

Pubs & bars 🍸
Bodega **22**
Market Bar **16**
Old Angel **17**
Pitcher and Piano **18**
Wax Bar **23**
Ye Olde Trip to Jerusalem **24**

Places in Nottingham

Market Square is the centre of Nottingham, about 600 yards almost directly north of the train station over the canal. The areas of the city of most interest to visitors fall either side of this north–south line passing through the Broadmarsh shopping centre. Beneath the shopping centre, though, **The City of Caves** ① *Drury Walk, Upper Level, Broadmarsh Shopping Centre, NG1 7LS, T0115-988 1955, www.cityofcaves.com, audio tours Mon-Fri 1030-1700 (last admission 1600), performance tours Sat-Sun, £6.50, child £5.50*, is quite an unusual visitor attraction. Large manmade sandstone caves are laid out to show how they have been used down the ages, up to their use as an air-raid shelter during the war.

Before Market Square, to the east, clustered around the church of St Mary's, the **Lace Market** area covers the site of Saxon Nottingham. Also here is **Contemporary Nottingham** ① *Weekday Cross, NG1 2GB, T0115-948 9750, Tue-Fri 1000-1900, Sat 1000-1800, Sun 1100-1700, free*, one of the largest contemporary art spaces in the UK. There are four galleries, as well as a café, and a range of events are on offer including talks, films and exhibitions. Nearby **St Mary's Church**, High Pavement, is home to the Nottingham Bach Choir, who rehearse on Tuesday evenings, and is worth a look in itself, especially the door in the south porch which frames a bronze Art Nouveau relief of Christ with the Virgin.

In the old **Shire Hall** ① *Galleries of Justice Experience, Shire Hall, High Pavement, Lace Market, NG1 1HN, T0115-952 0555, www.galleriesofjustice.org.uk, daily 0900-1700, £9.50, child £7.50, combined tickets with the City of Caves available*, dating from the mid-18th century, the **Galleries of Justice** is an interactive see-hear-and-smell show on the theme of crime and punishment, lent some authenticity by the original Victorian courtrooms and the old cells, where you're encouraged to "feel the atmosphere of 300 years of suffering seeping through the walls, bars and chains ..." Not for delicate sensibilities then, but most kids seem to love it.

North of St Mary's, St Mary's Gate and Stoney Street lead up into **Hockley**, another area of reclaimed and renovated old buildings that make for rewarding browsing. Heading 100 yards west out of Hockley brings you back to Market Square, dominated by the Baroque **Council House** on pedestrianized Smithy Row.

Anyone interested in the history of the city should head west from the Broadmarsh centre towards **Nottingham Castle** ① *off Friar La, NG1 6EL, T0115-915 3700, www.nottinghamcity.gov.uk, Mar-Oct Tue-Sun 1000-1700 (last admission 1600), Nov-Feb Tue-Sun 1000-1600 (last admission 1500), also open bank holiday Mon, £5.50, concessions £4, family £15, joint admission ticket for Nottingham Castle and The Museum of Nottingham Life is available*. It is home to a very fine collection of medieval alabaster carvings, a skill in which the city once excelled, as well as an intriguing array of Victorian paintings in a wonderful old gallery. In the Threads Gallery there are costumes from different periods, as well as shoes, hats and textiles. There are also historical displays and temporary exhibitions.

A stone's throw away, the **Museum of Nottingham Life** ① *Castle Blvd, NG7 1FB, T0115-915 3700, www.nottinghamcity.gov.uk, on the 1st weekend of every month 1100-1600 (last admission 1530), £2.50*, at **Brewhouse Yard** covers the social history of the city rather than its manufacturing pride, with mock-ups of shop fronts and a period living room and kitchen.

A small cave, **Mortimer's Hole** ① *T0115-915 3700, Tue-Sun 1100, 1400 and 1500 but call to confirm, £2.50, child £1.50*, under the castle can be seen on guided tours leaving from the top of the castle. Edward III's soldiers used the tunnel to enter the Castle and capture Roger de Mortimer in the 14th century. Northwest of the castle, the Roman Catholic Cathedral of **St Barnabas**, Derby Road, is another impressive piece of ecclesiastical design by Pugin.

Sherwood Forest National Nature Reserve

There's not much left of the forest made famous by Robin and his merry men but the 450 acres incorporate some areas of ancient native woodland. The tourist board make as much of it as they can, so it's well signposted off the M1. **Robyn Hode's Sherwode Exhibition** is at the **Sherwood Forest Country Park Visitor Centre** ① *Edwinstowe, NG21 9HN, T01623-823202*, a popular Victorian visitor attraction, admired by Washington Irving in 1835. The **Major Oak**, supposed trysting and trothing spot of Robin and Marian, its hollow trunk their lovenest, is about 800 years old, 20 minutes' walk from the Visitor Centre.

Some 12 miles north of Nottingham on the A60 (follow signs for Sherwood Forest from Junction 27 of the M1) is **Newstead Abbey** ① *Ravenshead, NG15 8GE, T01623-455900, www.newsteadabbey.org.uk, grounds open all year 0900-1600/dusk (whichever is sooner), house Sun tours 1200, 1300 and 1400 (subject to demand), £6 per car, additional £5 per person for a house tour*. Lord Byron lived here between 1808 and 1814, before selling his ancestral home (since 1540 and the dissolution of the monastery on the site) in 1818. Medieval cloisters, Great Hall, Byron's favourite clothes for you to try on, and a mock-up of his quarters are all decent enough diversions. The Gardens are the main event, though – over 300 acres of extraordinary parkland, with a variety of different gardens from around the world established on the lakeside.

Derby and around → *For listings, see pages 113-116.*

Not much to look at, except along the Georgian street called Friar Gate, home to the Pickford's House Museum and Old Derby Gaol, Derby has suffered as much as most other Midland towns at the hands of 1960s' redevelopers. That said, the pedestrianized area west and south of the cathedral can make for a pleasant enough wander around of an afternoon. A quarter of a mile to the north is the the Silk Mill, housed in the first factory in the country, and the start of a mile-long riverside walk to Darley Abbey, both part of a UNESCO World Heritage Site. Nearby are the neo classical splendours of Kedleston Hall. To the south of the city the extraordinary formal gardens at Melbourne Hall and the Donington Grand Prix Collection racetrack and racing car museum. To the northeast, the Amber Valley skirts abandoned mining country up to Hardwick Hall and Bolsover Castle. Northwest of the city, dignified old Ashbourne proudly proclaims itself the 'Gateway to Dovedale' and hence the Peak District as a whole.

Arriving in Derby

Getting there Regular **trains** connect Derby with Nottingham (25 minutes), Leicester (35 minutes) and on to London (two hours). Derby is about 130 miles from London, reachable in two hours by car, straight up the M1. It's also about one hour and 30 minutes from Leeds further up the M1. The big A38 heads straight into Birmingham, no more than 30 minutes away. **National Express** ① *www.nationalexpress.com*, run nine coaches a day to Derby from London Victoria (three hours 40 minutes).

Getting around Derby is a surprisingly large city. The centre is Market Place, about a mile and a half west of the **train** station (catch a **bus**, the walk's no fun) and a stone's throw from the grotty bus station in Morledge (a new bus station is under construction). But most of the sights worth seeing are within easy walking distance of each other.

Information Derby TIC ① *Assembly Rooms, Market Pl, DE1 3AH, T01332-255802, www.*
visitderby.co.uk, Mon-Sat 1000-1630. **Ashbourne TIC** ① *13 Market Pl, 13 Market Pl, DE6*
1EU, T01335-343666, www.visitashbourne.co.uk, Mar-Oct Mon-Sat 0930-1730, Nov-Feb
Mon-Sat 1000-1700. **Amber Valley TIC** ① *Town Hall, Market Pl, Ripley, DE5 3SZ, T01773-*
841485, www.visitambervalley.co.uk.

History

One of the five major towns of the Danelaw (alongside Nottingham and Leicester), Derby
became an important local centre in the Middle Ages. It was only in the 18th century,
though, that the city's fortunes really began take off, with the success of the Lombes' silk
mill, arguably the first factory in the country (now the Industrial Museum). Chinaware
(Royal Crown Derby) and the Midland Railway enhanced its industrial base, and in the
early years of the 20th century Rolls Royce moved their works to the city. The Derwent
Valley from Cromford to Derby was declared a World Heritage Site by UNESCO thanks to its
starring role in the dawn of the Industrial Revolution and the machine age.

Places in Derby

By car, Derby shows itself to its best advantage when approached from Ashbourne and
the west down the red-brick Georgian street called Friar Gate, the opposite side of the city
from the station. On Friar Gate itself, the **Derby Gaol** ① *50-51 Friar Gate, DE1 1DF, T0800-*
027 7928, www.derbygaol.com, reveals what lay in store for the offenders during the city's
industrial heyday. A few doors down, the **Pickford's House Museum** ① *41 Friar Gate, DE1*
1DA, T01332-715181, www.derbymuseums.org, Tue-Sat 1000-1700, Sun 1300-1600, free,
home of the architect Joseph Pickford has been restored to its c.1800 appearance. Some
rooms have been furnished as they might have been when the Pickford family lived in
the house. Others contain displays of costume and textiles and also the Frank Bradley
collection of toy theatres.

At the end of Friar Gate, where it meets The Wardwick, a left turn down Curzon Street
arrives at the Strand and the **Derby Museum and Art Gallery** ① *The Strand, DE1 1BS,*
T01332-641901, www.derbymuseums.org, Tue-Sat 1000-1700, Sun 1300-1600, free. This
holds a fine collection of Joseph Wright of Derby's paintings, as well as a ceramics gallery,
and displays on the local archaeology, history, wildlife and geology.

A few steps down St James Street from here leads into Market Place, from where it's
a short walk up Iron Gate to the cathedral. With its airy 18th-century neo classical nave,
designed by Gibb and restored by Comper, and a medieval tower over the entrance porch,
Derby Cathedral ① *18-19 Iron Gate, DE1 3GP, T01332-341201, www.derbycathedral.org,*
Mon-Friday 0800-1800, Thu 0800-1930, Sat 0900-1800, Sun 0730-1930, is delightful but only
just deserves the name. Inside, highlights include the monument to the formidable Bess of
Hardwick (1607) and Robert Bakewell's elegant early 18th-century ironwork.

A three-minute walk from the cathedral down Sowter Road arrives at the **Silk Mill**. This
UNESCO World Heritage Site and 18th-century silk mill on the banks of the Derwent is
currently closed for redevelopment. Built between 1717 and 1721 for the Lombe brothers,
it was hard-hit in the 19th century by overseas competition and ceased production in 1908.

A mile away by footpath along the river, the **Darley Abbey and Park** ① *www.*
darleyabbey.com, is also part of the World Heritage Site, the remains (much altered and
redeveloped) of a late-18th-century factory village developed by Thomas Evans.

About a mile south of Market Place, on the road to Melbourne, the **Royal Crown Derby
Visitor Centre** ① *194 Osmaston Rd, DE23 8JZ, T01332-712833, www.royalcrownderby.co.uk,*

factory tours Tue-Thu 1100 and 1300, Fri 1100, £5, concessions £4.75, offers factory tours, and there's a shop and a small museum.

Derwent and Amber Valleys

North and upstream of Derby the Derwent and Amber Valleys embrace the towns of Belper, Ripley, Heanor and Alfreton. The area's manufacturing heritage can be explored at the magnificent **Belper North Mill** ⓘ *Derwent Valley Visitor Centre, Bridgefoot, Belper, DE56 1YD, T01773-880474, www.belpernorthmill.org, Mar-Oct Wed-Sun and Bank Holiday Mond 1300-1700, Nov-Feb Sat-Sun 1300-1700, £3.50, child £2*, once a state-of-the-art water-powered and fire-proof cotton mill. The huge iron-framed building was completed in the early 1800s by the son of Jedediah Strutt, whose 1786 building had been destroyed in a fire. Models and a few original spinning machines can be seen.

The **National Heritage Corridor** ⓘ *T01773-841485, www.nationalheritage corridor.org. uk*, is a celebration of one of the country's hardest worked rivers: the Derwent. Particularly attractive woodland stretches can be found at **Whatstandwell** (yachtswoman Ellen MacArthur's home town) and **Ambergate**. The river runs on through Belper and down into Derby.

Seven miles north of Alfreton, just east of Junctions 28 and 29 on the M1, **Hardwick Old Hall** ⓘ *(EH), S44 5QJ, T01246-850431, www.english-heritage.org.uk, see website for opening hours, £5.20, child £3.10, family £13.50*, is the ruin of Bess of Hardwick's Elizabethan family home and there are spectacular views from the roof. Next door to the Hardwick Old Hall is the palatial Elizabethan residence that Bess built for herself in the 1590s, **Hardwick New Hall** ⓘ *(NT), S44 5QJ, T01246-850430, www.nationaltrust.org.uk/hardwick, see website for opening hours, gardens only £5.45, child £2.65, family £13.60, house and garden £10.90, child £5.45, family £27.25*. Highlights of its interior are the wealth of 16th-century furniture, tapestries and needlework. Outside, the glorious gardens stretching over to the Old Hall give superb views over the M1 and surrounding countryside.

Also visible from the M1, and particularly spectacular when floodlit at night, **Bolsover Castle** ⓘ *(EH), off junctions 29 or 30 on the M1, in Bolsover 6 miles east of Chesterfield, Castle St, S44 6PR, T01246-822844, www.english-heritage.org.uk, see website for opening hours, £8.50, child £5.10, family £22.10*, was built in the 17th century as a romantic love nest on the site of a medieval castle. It was constructed by Sir Charles Cavendish as a retreat from the world, where he could indulge his fondness for all things chivalric and medieval. The Venus Fountain in the grounds, featuring cherubs relieving themselves into the water below, is typical of the playful tone Sir Charles wanted his guests to appreciate.

Ashbourne and Dovedale

Some 11 miles northwest of Derby up the A52, Ashbourne is a quaint red-brick town, proudly proclaiming itself the 'Gateway to Dovedale'. Its preserved medieval street pattern and Georgian rebuilding give the place its peculiar charm. St John Street is the most interesting architecturally, with its gallows cross still standing. Ashbourne was dubbed 'Oakbourne' by George Eliot in her novel *Adam Bede*. She also described St Oswald's Church with its beautiful spire as the "finest mere parish church in the kingdom". The interior is full of surprises, including carvings, and fine stained glass, and the Cockayne chapel commemorating two centuries-worth of local bigwigs. With its cobbled market place and old pubs, Ashbourne does make a good base from which to set off into the Peak District.

South of Derby

To the south of Derby, a couple of very grand houses are worth seeking out. **Kedleston Hall** ① (NT), DE22 5JH, T01332-842191, www.nationaltrust.org.uk/kedleston-hall, see website for opening hours, park and garden only £3.95, child £1.95, family £9.95, whole property £8.90, child £4.40, family £22.30, winter £1.00, child 50p, is a beautiful neo classical mansion built in the mid-18th century for the Curzons, its interiors designed by Robert Adam. There's also an Eastern Museum displaying the loot acquired by Lord Curzon as Viceroy of India at the turn of the last century.

Not far to the east, the village of **Melbourne** is also worth a detour: the church is a remarkably complete (especially on the inside) Norman church that looks like a small cathedral. It has three towers, the central one a 17th-century belltower with 12 bells. Inside are superb carvings, a sheela-na-gig or pagan fertility symbol, and Australian flags. The latter can be explained at **Melbourne Hall** ① Church Sq, DE73 8EN, T01332-862502, www.melbournehall.com, hall and gardens daily in Aug (except for the first 3 Mon), gardens 1330-1730, hall 1400-1615, gardens Apr-Jul and Sep Wed, Sat, Sun and Bank Holiday Mon 1330-1730gardens £4.50, child £3.50, Hall £4.00, child £3, Hall and gardens £6.50, child £4.50, with its formal, well-tended and little-altered French gardens designed in the late 17th-century in the style of Le Notre by Henry Wise and George London (who also worked at Hampton Court, Longleat, Petworth and Chatsworth). This was once the home of Victorian PM William Lamb Lord Melbourne, troubled husband of Byron's lover Caroline Lamb.

At **Donington** ① Donington Park Grand Prix Collection, Castle Donington, DE74 2RP, T01332-811027, www.donington-park.co.uk, daily 1000-1700 (last admission 1600), £10, child £4, you'll find one of the country's most extensive collections of Formula 1 cars at an historic racetrack just off the M1. It features more than 130 of the snarling machines, dating from the early 20th century to the present day.

Nottinghamshire and Derbyshire listings

For hotel and restaurant price codes and other relevant information, see pages 9-12.

⊖ Where to stay

Nottingham *p105, map p106*
££££-£££ Langar Hall, Church La, Langar, NG13 9HG, T01949-860559, www.langarhall. com. Regency house with bags of character in a beautiful village setting and acres of parkland, some way southeast of the city. Recommended.
£££ Lace Market Hotel, 29-31 High Pavement, NG1 1HE, T0115-852 3232, www.thefinessecollection.com/lacemarket. In a great location offering good rooms in 5 categories and access to a nearby healthclub. Decent restaurant and bar on site.
£££-££ Mercure Nottingham City Centre, George St, NG1 3BP, T0115-959 9777, www.mercurenottingham.com. Good, central chain offering with all the facilities you'd expect including a small gym.
£££-££ Walton's Hotel, Bar & Restaurant, 2 North Rd, The Park Estate, NG7 1AG, T0115-947 5215, www.waltonshotel.co.uk. Small hotel walking distance to sights with good food and quiet, comfortable rooms.
£ Igloo Backpackers Hostel, 110 Mansfield Rd, NG1 3HL, T0115-947 5250, www.igloo hostel.co.uk. Dorms and private rooms, and a well equipped kitchen. Good location.

Derby and around *p109*
££££ Callow Hall, Mappleton Rd, Ashbourne, DE6 2AA, T01335-300900, www.callowhall.co.uk. The smart option, a hotel about a mile west of the town in a large Victorian house. Good English food in the restaurant.
£££ Cathedral Quarter Hotel, 16 St Mary's Gate, Derby, DE1 3JR, T01332-546080, www. thefinessecollection.com/cathedralquarter. Central hotel in a converted Grade II listed building that formerly housed council offices. Good restaurant and there's a spa.

£££-££ Station Hotel, Station Rd, Ashbourne, DE6 1AA, T01335-300035, www.stationhotel.eu. Quite a large hotel in a Victorian house in the middle of town. The Tissington Trail starts over the road from the hotel.
£ Beechenhill Farm, Ashbourne, DE6 2BD, T01335-310274, www.beechenhill.co.uk. An organic working farm with 2 double B&B rooms and 2 self-catering cottages (sleeping 2 and 6 people, **££££**, more reasonably priced the longer you stay) with superb views and colourful garden.

⑦ Restaurants

Nottingham *p105, map p106*
£££-££ Hart's, Standard Hill, Park Row, NG1 6GN, T0115-988 1900, www.harts nottingham.co.uk. A sophisticated ambience, professional service and superior modern cuisine can be enjoyed here.
£££-££ Mem Saab, 12 Maid Marian Way, NG1 6HS, T0115-957 0009, www.mem-saab.co.uk. A good Indian restaurant in the middle of town, boasts stylish decor.
£££-££ World Service, Newdigate House, Castle Gate, NG1 6AF, T0115-847 5587, www.worldservicerestaurant.com. Fresh, seasonal food, the menu warns some dishes may contain lead shot! A Georgian house with a garden and sumptuous surroundings. Booking essential, weekday set menu good value.
££ 4550 Miles from Delhi, Maid Marion Way, 41 Mount St, NG1 6HE, T0115-9475 111, www.4550.co.uk/nottingham. Deservedly popular restaurant serving delicious North Indian food.
££ Emilio's Greek Restaurant, 8 High St, Arnold, NG5 7DZ, T0115-926 2550, www.emiliosgreekrestaurant.co.uk. Delicious, traditional Greek food, and friendly service. Can get very busy at weekends.
££ French Living, 27 King St, NG1 2AY, T0115-958 5885, www.frenchliving.co.uk.

Very good value (especially the *plat du jour* at lunchtime) rustic French fare in the middle of town. 5 mins' walk from Market Square. Hosts raclette evenings.

££ Jamie's Italian, 24-26 Low Pavement, NG1 7DL, T0115-822 1421, www.jamieoliver. com/italian. Jamie Oliver's restaurant serves filling Italian fare, good option for those with kids.

££ Laguna Tandoori, 43 Mount St, NG1 6HE, T0115-941 1632, www.laguna tandoori.co.uk. A reliable north Indian restaurant that's been around for years.

££ Royal Thai, 189 Mansfield Rd, NG1 3FS, T0115-948 3001, www.royalthairestaurant. co.uk. Reliable Thai restaurant about 20 mins' walk from the middle of town uphill.

Derby and around *p109*

£££ Darley's on the River, Darley Abbey Mill, Derby, DE22 1DZ, T01332-364987, www.darleys.com. Probably the smartest restaurant in Derby, with an ambitious but accomplished menu. Lunch menus are good value. A 20-min walk along the river.

££ Lamplight, 4 Victoria Sq, Ashbourne, DE6 1GG, T01335-342279, www.the-lamplight.co.uk. Family-run restaurant in a former 15th-century coaching inn. Filling and elegant dishes, à la carte and set menus.

££ Le Bistrot Pierre, 18 Friar Gate Derby, DE1 1BX, T01332-370470, www.lebistrot pierre.co.uk. A reliable chain restaurant serving up French-inspired dishes.

🕦 Pubs and bars

Nottingham *p105, map p106*

Bodega, 23 Pelham St, NG1 2ED, T0845-413 4444, www.bodeganottingham.com. Formerly **The Social**, this bar hosts gigs and club nights. One of the places to come for live music.

Market Bar, 16-22 Goose Gate, NG1 1FF, T0115-988 1707, T0115-959 9777. Very popular with the more happening section of the city's student population, has a good range of music playing.

Old Angel, 7 Stoney St, Lace Market, NG1 1LG, T0115-947 6735, www.theoldangel. com. A grubby rock pub that serves food and has a live music venue upstairs. You'll either love it or hate it.

Pitcher and Piano, High Pavement, Lace Market, NG1 1HN, T0115-958 6081. A chain bar but quite out of the ordinary, established in the late 90s in a converted Unitarian church.

Wax Bar, 27 Broad St, Hockley, NG1 3AP, T0115-959 0007, www.waxbar-nottingham. co.uk. Small live music bar, Mon is curry night.

Ye Olde Trip to Jerusalem, Castle Rd, NG1 6AD, T0115-947 3171, www.tripto jerusalem.com. Reputedly the oldest pub in Britain, where the Crusaders gathered before setting off to bash up the infidels. Today it's an interesting place, gouged out of the rock beneath the castle. Offers cellar tours, see website for details.

Clubs

As well as many of the bars listed above, where flyers abound, possible options include:

Arriba Club, 28 St Jame's St, NG1 6FG, T0115-947 6695. For mainstream dance sounds every night of the week. Popular late-night drinking spot.

Gatecrasher, Elite Building, 2 Queen St, NG1 2BL, T0115-910 1101, www.gatecrasher. com. Owned by the international clubbing brand. Set over 4 floors this is the place to come for House and Dance music.

Derby and around *p109*

Derby is famous for its pride in and devotion to real ale and several good pubs pull pints of the stuff at its best.

The Brunswick, 1 Railway Terr, Derby, DE1 2RU, T01332-290677, www.brunswick derby.co.uk. One of the city's most popular real ale pubs, with an exceptional variety in barrels and on the pumps, very close to the railway station.

The Flower Pot, 23-25 King St, Derby, DE1 3DZ, T01332-204955, www.the-flowerpot-pub.co.uk. Just round the corner of the

cathedral, with a small beer garden, lots of books, some very fine ales and live music.
The Smithfield, Meadow Rd, Derby, DE1 2BH, T01332-370429, www.thesmithfield. moonfruit.com. On the banks of the Derwent, next to the old cattle market, another pub with about 10 different real ales on offer.
Ye Olde Dolphin, 6 Queen St, Derby, DE1 3DL, T01332-267711. A beamed 16th-century pub within walking distance of the cathedral. Claims to be the most haunted pub in town.
Ye Olde Vaults, 21 Market Pl, Ashbourne, DE6 1EU, T01335-346127. Another rambling, popular old pub right at the bottom of the market square in Ashbourne.

⊙ Entertainment

Nottingham *p105, map p106*
Cinema
Broadway Cinema, 14-18 Broad St, NG1 3AL, T0115-952 6611, www.broadway.org. uk. Indie and foreign films, also has a café.
Cineworld Cinema The Corner House, 29 Forman St, NG1 4AA, T0844-815 7747, www.cineworld.co.uk. Hollywood blockbusters in **The Corner House**, a large leisure and entertainment complex opposite the Theatre Royal and Royal Concert Hall.

Music
Capital FM Arena, Bolero Sq, The Lace Market, NG1 1LA, T0843-373 3000, www.capitalfmarena.com. Venue for big names on tour.

Theatre
Nottingham Playhouse, Wellington Circus, NG1 5AF, T0115-947 4361, www.nottinghamplayhouse.co.uk. Contemporary drama and dance.
Theatre Royal, Theatre Sq, NG1 5ND, T0115-589 5555, www.trch.co.uk. For West End musicals, ballet and classical concerts.

⊙ Shopping

Nottingham *p105, map p106*
You can do a lot of shopping in Nottingham with 6 department stores, 4 covered shopping malls and High Street and independent shops and boutiques. The largest covered shopping malls are the **Victoria Centre** and the **Broadmarsh Centre**. Hockley, the area north of Carlton St, is where many of the city's specialist and independent retailers have set up shop, while King's Walk, a few steps west of the Victoria Centre is another place for boutiques and jewellers. There are also a range of shops south of the County Hall in Market Square.

⊙ What to do

Nottingham *p105, map p106*
Art galleries
Angel Row Gallery, Central Library Building, 3 Angel Row, NG1 6HP, T0115-915 2873. Innovative public space with interesting temporary exhibitions by contemporary artists.
The Bonnington Gallery (Bonnington Building) and The 1851 Gallery (Waverley Building), Nottingham Trent University, Dryden St, NG7 4HF. Bonnington Gallery, T0115-848 8268, Mon-Fri 1000-1700, 1851 Gallery T0115-848 6131, Mon-Thu 0730-2100, Fri 730-2030. Have exhibitions of contemporary art and performances.
Djanogly Art Gallery, Lakeside Arts Centre, University of Nottingham, NG7 2RD, www.lakesidearts.org.uk. Nottingham Unversity's art gallery, with changing exhibitions of contemporary art as well as displays from the university's collection.

Sport
National Ice Centre, Bolero Sq, The Lace Market, NG1 1LA, T0843-373 3000, www.national-ice-centre.com. Home to the Nottingham Panthers Ice Hockey team, with 2 large rinks for skating on.

National Water Sports Centre, Holme Pierrepont, Adbolton La, Holme Pierrepont, NG12 2LU, T0115-982 4707, www.nwscnotts.com. 3 miles east of the city centre, in 250 acres of parkland.
Nottingham Forest Football Club, The City Ground, Pavilion Rd, NG2 5FJ, T0115-982 4444, www.nottinghamforest.co.uk.
Nottingham Tennis Centre, University Boulevard, NG7 2QH, T0115-876 1600.
Nottinghamshire County Cricket Club, Trent Bridge, Bridgford Rd, West Bridgford, NG2 6AG, T0115-982 3000, www.nottsccc.co.uk. 1 of the 6 Test Match venues, with Notts CCC playing Apr-Sep.

⊖ Transport

Nottingham *p105, map p106*
Bicycle
Bunneys Bikes, 97 Carrington St, NG1 7FE, T0115-947 2713, www.bunneysbikes.com.

Bus
Trent Barton buses, www.trentbarton.co.uk, run the regular direct service to **Derby** (35 mins) from Victoria bus station. **National Express**, www.nationalexpress.com, run regular sevices from Broad Marsh Bus Station to **Birmingham Digbeth** (1 hr 25 mins to 2 hrs 1 mins) and to **London Victoria** (3 hrs 10 mins). There is also a regular service to **Leicester** (1 hr) and a service to **Leeds** (2 hrs 10 mins).

Car
Avis, Arndale Centre, Maid Marian Way, NG1 6AE, T0844-544 6085, www.avis.co.uk; **Enterprise**, Suite 1, Heston Hse, Meadow La, NG2 3HQ, T0115-985 0999, www.enterprise.co.uk; **Pacer Vehicle Rental**, 601 Woodborough Rd, NG3 5GG, T0115-969 3166.

Taxi
Streamline Taxis, 109a Mansfield Rd, NG1 3FQ, T0115-924 2499; **Yellow Cars**, 8 Pavillion Building, Pavillion Rd, NG2 5FG, T0115-981 8181, www.yellowcars.net.

Train
Cross Country Trains, www.crosscountrytrains.co.uk, run the regular direct services to **Birmingham New Street** (1 hr 25 mins), **Derby** (25-30 mins) and the direct hourly service to **Manchester Oxford Road** (1 hr 55 mins). **East Midlands Trains**, www.crosscountrytrains.co.uk, run the frequent direct service to **Leicester** (25-45 mins) and to **London St Pancras** (1 hr 45 mins to 2 hrs).

⊕ Directory

Nottingham *p105, map p106*
Hospital Nottingham City Hospital, Hucknall Rd, NG5 1PB, T0115-969 1169.
Police Nottingham Police HQ, Sherwood Lodge Arnold, NG5 8PP, T101, www.nottinghamshire.police.uk. **Post office** Queen St, NG1 2BN.

Leicestershire

Leicestershire is a quiet, comfortable and undramatic sort of county. Undemonstrative in landscape or manner, it's considerably enlivened by the multi-cultural and reinvigorated city at its heart. Leicester itself rewards a visit not with its architecture or streetscape, but with its upbeat attitude and a clutch of innovative sights. Most prominent of these is the National Space Centre, a lottery-funded Millennium project that looks set to last. With its 'Golden Mile' of curry houses and thriving arts scene, Leicester has little reason to be nostalgic for the days when it was dominated by light and heavy industry. It recently made the headlines when a skeleton found under a council car park was proved to be that of Richard III.

The countryside around the city harbours a few surprises, especially the rolling hills or wolds beyond and en route to Melton Mowbray, home of the British pork pie.

Leicester → *For listings, see pages 122-124.*

Somewhat akin to the rings of the planet Saturn, Leicester is surrounded by both a notoriously tricky traffic system and a thick miasma of southern snobbery, which tends all too readily to dismiss it as a run-down manufacturing town of little cultural significance. In fact, Leicester has from Roman times been recognized as the very centre of England – the furthest point from any coast or border – and has regularly played a pivotal historical role. The city contains a number of interesting buildings and monuments, and – indicative of a return from a period of industrial decline – a recent rash of sharp little restaurants and bars. With its Asian community making up almost a third of its 329,900 population, Leicester is also one of the very best examples of England's modern, integrated multi-cultural society. In particular, the shopkeepers and restaurateurs of the city's Belgrave Road, or 'Golden Mile', have created a vibrant streak of Indian life that is now as much a part of the city as its famous 700-year-old covered market.

Arriving in Leicester

Getting there East Midlands Airport ① *www.eastmidlandsairport.com*, and **Birmingham International Airport** ① *www.birminghamairport.co.uk*, are, respectively, 30 and 45 minutes away by car. There are several trains every hour on the **East Midlands** service from London St Pancras (one hour and 10 minutes by the fast service). Leicester is 100 miles, or about two hours, from London **by car**, straight up the M1. The M1 is also linked, at junction 21, with the M69 west to Coventry, which is itself linked to the M6 for destinations in the West Midlands and the Northwest. For the city centre, turn off the M1 at junction 21 onto the A5460 Narborough Road, before turning right onto St Augustine Road, immediately crossing the river to the car park at St Nicholas Circle. **National Express** ① *www.nationalexpress.com*, offers services throughout the country from St Margaret's Bus Station, just north of the city centre. ▸▸ *See Transport, page 124, for more details.*

Getting around The centre of Leicester is encompassed, unprepossessingly, by the busy A594 ring road. Inside this circle, the city is small enough to negotiate on foot. However, a trip out to the Belgrave Road area or the National Space Centre will definitely require the use of a bus for at least one stretch of the journey.

Information Visit Leicester ① *51 Gallowtree Gate, LE1 5AD, T0116-299 4444, www. visitleicester.info, Mon-Sat 1000-1800, Sun 1100-1700.* The website is worth checking out before your visit.

History

The name Leicester comes from 'Legro Ceaster', meaning the Roman 'camp on the River Legro', now called the River Soar. The settlement, first established in AD48, stood near the crossroads of two great Roman thoroughfares, Watling Street and the Fosse Way. Another Roman road, the Via Devana, is preserved as a pedestrian street called New Walk, whilst the remains of the second century Roman baths can be seen at the Jewry Wall Museum. Leicester was an important town under both the Danish and Norman invaders and a pleasant park now surrounds the mound or motte of the 11th-century castle.

The city's relationship with its kings has been fraught. In 1264, the sixth Earl of Leicester, Simon de Montfort – whose statue adorns the 19th-century clock tower at the city centre and after whom one of the city's two universities is named – led a revolt against Henry III and briefly set up the first English parliament in the city. The 11th Earl, John of Gaunt, was the father of Henry of Lancaster, who defeated Richard II to become Henry IV. In 1485, the Wars of the Roses came to an end when Richard III rode out of Leicester to his death at the Battle of Bosworth Field – his monument may be found in the chancel of the cathedral. In 1645, during the next civil war, Leicester's brave and vastly outnumbered citizens held out for five days against the royalist troops of Charles I, only two weeks before the king was finally defeated by Cromwell at the Battle of Naseby.

In more recent times, Leicester has been renowned for its hosiery trade, one of the chief reasons for the influx in the 1970s of Indian workers, many of whom came not from the subcontinent, but from the disaster that was Idi Amin's Uganda. Computerization led to huge job losses in this industry at the end of the 20th century, just as the invention of the hand-powered knitting frames in the 19th century had led to job losses then, provoking a young Leicester apprentice called Ned Ludlam to smash a couple of these hated machines, henceforth forever lumbering technophobes the world over with the term 'Luddite'.

Places in Leicester
From a distance, the rocket tower of the **National Space Centre** ⓘ *2 miles north of the city centre, Exploration Dr, LE4 5NS, T0845-605 2001, www.spacecentre.co.uk, Tue-Fri 1000-1600, Sat-Sun 1000-1700, during school holidays daily 1000-1700, £13, child £11*, enveloped in a hi-tech, silver sheath, looks like an enormous sci-fi maggot. Once inside, the centre is divided into different zones exploring different aspects of space travel and the universe. Highlights include a replica of the Columbus space station, showing how astronauts eat, sleep and go to the loo in space, and a Soyuz T space capsule used to ferry astronauts to the Mir space station.

Coming back down to earth, the nearby **Abbey Pumping Station** ⓘ *T0116-299 5111, www.abbeypumpingstation.org, Feb-Oct daily 1100-1630, free*, is a Victorian sewage works that has been reinvented as Leicester's Museum of Science and Technology

The '**Golden Mile**' is actually best seen in the evening, when it turns into a neon-lit promenade, a place to window shop and meet friends, before diving into one of the many different eateries for a bite or a full-blown meal. See Eating and Shopping below.

The diminutive **Cathedral** ⓘ *7 Peacock La, LE1 5PZ, T0116-261 5200, www.cathedral. leicester.anglican.org*, is an essentially Victorian structure built over the remains of a much older church. The chancel contains the floor memorial to Richard III – with his hunched back, the inspiration for the Humpty Dumpty nursery rhyme – and the engravings on the modern glass doors illustrate the Escape from Egypt. There are plans to re-inter the newly discovered remains of Richard III in the cathedral. The **Guildhall** ⓘ *Guildhall La, LE1 5FQ, T0116-253 2569, free*, right beside the cathedral, is a beautifully preserved 14th-century half-timbered structure, the venue for many of the most significant events in Leicester's history and still in use for some civic functions to this day. It is also hosting an exhibition on Richard III until 2014. Continue back along the High Street and over the A594 to find the **Jewry Wall Museum** ⓘ *St Nicholas Circle, LE1 4LB, T0116-225 4971, Feb-Oct 1100-1630, free*, site of the moderately exciting remains of the Roman baths and display of local archaeology, that includes two genuinely impressive Roman mosaics.

From here, head a few steps north to the **Guru Nanak Sikh Museum** ⓘ *9 Holy Bones, LE1 4LJ, T0116-262 8606, www.thesikhmuseum.co.uk, museum Thu 1300-1600, Sat 1900-2030, or by appointment, free*, a working Sikh Gurdwara open daily for worship and free food, with a museum of Sikh history upstairs. A short walk south takes you to the castle gardens, containing the mound of the Norman castle and the **Newarke Houses**

Museum ① *The Newarke, LE2 7BY, T0116-225 4980, Mon-Sat 1000-1700, Sun 1100-1700, free*, home to an eclectic collection of such things as clocks, toys and Indian embroidery, including the portrait and various possessions of Daniel Lambert, an enormously fat 19th-century gentleman, who tipped the scales at 52 stone 11 lbs. Just behind the

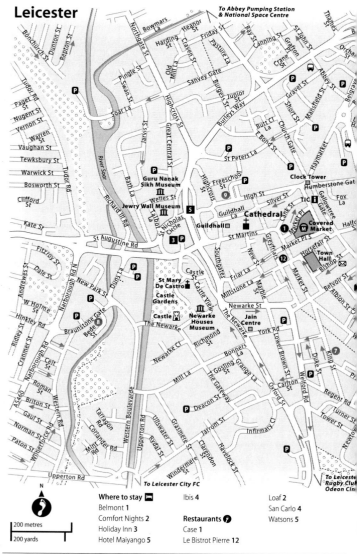

Leicester

To Abbey Pumping Station & National Space Centre

Where to stay 🛏
Belmont **1**
Comfort Nights **2**
Holiday Inn **3**
Hotel Maiyango **5**

Ibis **4**

Restaurants 🍴
Case **1**
Le Bistrot Pierre **12**

Loaf **2**
San Carlo **4**
Watsons **5**

To Leicester City FC

200 metres
200 yards

museum, the church of **St Mary de Castro** ① *T0116-287 0729, www.stmarydecastro. org.uk, Mon-Fri 1200-1400, Sat 1400-1600, phone T077-6997 6151 to arrange to visit at other times*, with its exceptional Norman chancel, was the site of the 14th-century poet Geoffrey Chaucer's second marriage.

Pubs & bars ①
Ale Wagon **14**
King's Head **7**
Left Bank **8**
Orange Tree **9**

Returning once more over the A594, look in at the **Jain Centre** ① *32 Oxford St, LE1 5XU, T0116-254 1150, daily, free*, in the converted congregational chapel on Oxford Street, the only Jain temple in the Western world, which contains some fine imported Indian carvings. Walk past the gargantuan Leicester City Council offices onto King Street and amble down leafy New Walk to the **New Walk Museum & Art Gallery** ① *53 New Walk, LE1 7EA, T0116-225 4900, Mon-Sat 1000-1700, Sun 1100-1700, free*, which has exhibits on natural history, ancient Egypt, and also a a celebrated collection of German Expressionist paintings.

Around Leicester

Melton Mowbray, 15 miles northeast of Leicester, is an unassuming Midlands market town, justly famous for its mighty pork pies, beloved of the horsey set and cheese-eaters. One of the many places (and also one of the most likely) that Stilton cheese is supposed to have originated is at Wymondham, six miles west of the town. The **Carnegie Museum** ① *Thorpe End, LE13 1RB, T0116-305 3860, www.leics. gov.uk/meltonmuseum.htm, Tue-Sat 1000-1630*, features displays on local history. **St Mary's Church**, with its extraordinary array of celestory windows (48 of them in all), is also worth a look. If you want to hunt down a pork pie, **Ye Olde Pork Pie Shoppe** ① *8-10 Nottingham St, LE13 1NW, T01664-482068, www.porkpie.co.uk*, which is also a tourist information point, should be more than happy to help.

North of Melton, the A607 heads up towards **Grantham**. Any turn left westwards leads up into delightful undiscovered villages in the wolds, a surprising area of rolling hills overlooking the Vale of Belvoir (pronounced *Beaver*) and giving beautiful views over Leicestershire. **Belvoir Castle**

① Grantham, NG32 1PE, T01476-871002, www.belvoircastle.com, entry to the Castle is by guided tour only at 1115, 1315 and 1515 on the dates shown on the website, gardens are open from 1100-1700 only on the dates shown on the website, £15, child £8, garden only £8, child £5, the home of the Duke of Rutland, is an imposing exercise in Regency romantic medievalism, full of remarkable paintings and once the scene of very grand house parties.

Some 15 miles southeast of Leicester, **Market Harborough** is another even less assuming Midlands market town. The attractive old part of town, including a grammar school founded in the reign of James I, clusters beneath the impressive broach spire of St Dionysius. Nine miles east of the town, **Rockingham Castle** ① Rockingham, LE16 8TH, T01536-770240, www.rockinghamcastle.com, Mar-May Sun and bank holiday Mon, Jun-Sep also on Tue, gardens 1200-1700, castle 1300-1700, £9.50, child £5.50, is an impressive Tudor house built within the walls of a Norman castle. Charles Dickens was inspired to model Chesney Wold in *Bleak House* on the place and today the interiors and wild gardens (including a 400-year-old elephant hedge) and their superb views are still worth a look.

Leicestershire listings

For hotel and restaurant price codes and other relevant information, see pages 9-12.

🛏 Where to stay

Leicester *p118, map p120*

£££-££ Hotel Maiyango, 13-21 St Nicholas Pl, LE1 4LD, T0116-251 8898, www.maiyango.com. Central boutique hotel with a good restaurant (see below).

££ Belmont Hotel, de Montfort St, LE1 7GR, T0116-254 4773, www.belmonthotel.co.uk. This country house hotel is just 5 mins' walk from the city centre along the tree-lined New Walk, an old Roman road. Also offers theatre packages.

££ Holiday Inn, 129 St Nicholas Circle, LE1 5LX, T0871-942 9048, www.ihg.com. Next door to the remains of the Roman baths, this modern hotel is built on the site of a Roman temple to the Persian god Mithras. Conveniently located for the motorway and the city centre, facilities include a gym and indoor pool.

££ Ibis Hotel, St George's Way, LE1 1PL, T0116-248 7200, www.ibis.com. Right next door to the railway station, this functional, barn of a building offers Leicester's best-value accommodation.

££-£ Comfort Nights, 23-25 Loughborough Rd, LE4 5LJ, T0116-268 2626, www.comfort nights-kabalous.co.uk. At the north end of the 'Golden Mile', this well-appointed hotel features the amazingly kitsch *Kabalou* restaurant, serving Indian food in an interior of mock Gothic-Indian-Egyptian-Greek design.

🍴 Restaurants

Leicester *p118, map p120*

£££-££ Maiyango, 13-21 St Nicholas Pl, LE1 4LD, T0116-251 8898, www.maiyango. com. Set lunch and dinner menus using seasonal produce, locally sourced where possible. Also offers cocktail-making classes. Recommended.

££ The Case, 4-6 Hotel St, St.Martins, LE1 5AW, T0116-251 7675, www.thecase.co.uk. Champagne bar on the ground floor and a European-style restaurant upstairs. Set lunch menus and early dinners menus are good value.

££ Le Bistrot Pierre, 8-10 Millstone La, LE1 5JN, T0116-262 7927, www.lebistrot pierre.co.uk. A popular chain restaurant serving French food. The lunch and Long Weekend menus are good value.

££ San Carlo, 38-40 Granby St, LE1 1DE, T0116-251 9332, www.sancarlo.co.uk. The nearest thing to *La Caprice* in Leicester. White tiles, blue neon, chrome and high quality Italian food.

Golden Mile

££ Chaat House, 108 Belgrave Rd, LE4 5AT, T0116-266 0513. A little different, an intimate den serving many different versions of the eponymous North Indian snack.

££ The Curry Fever, 139 Belgrave Rd, LE4 6AS, T0116-266 2941, www.thecurryfever.co.uk. The menu here contains few surprises, but is very highly regarded.

££-£ Bobbies, 154 Belgrave Rd, LE4 5AT, T0116-266 2448, www.eatatbobbys.com. Another sweetmart and vegetarian restaurant definitely worth a visit, to eat-in or takeaway.

££-£ Sharmilee, 71 Belgrave Rd, LE4 6AS, T0116-266 8471, www.sharmilee.co.uk. Closed Mon. A sweetmart, a buffet, and a restaurant serving excellent veggie dishes.

Pubs and bars

Leicester *p118, map p120*
The Ale Wagon, 27 Rutland St, LE1 1RE, T0116-262 3330, www.alewagon.co.uk. A traditional pub with no food but good real ales and the occasional beer festival.

The King's Head, 36 King St, LE1 6RL, T0116-254 8240, www.thekingsleicester.co.uk. Leicester's most relaxed boozer. Soothing green benches, big wooden tables and newspapers, a selection of real ales and decent food for a very mixed, laid-back clientele.

Left Bank, 26 Braunstone Gate, LE3 5LG, T0116-255 2422. This was one of the first trendy bars to spring up in the popular little nightlife enclave west of the river. Serves excellent fresh food.

The Orange Tree, 99 High St, LE1 4JB, T0116-223 5256, www.orangetree.co.uk. Mellow wooden floors and wooden tables, an easy-going crowd, a wide range of cocktails and happy hours throughout the week.

Entertainment

Leicester *p118, map p120*
Cinema
Odeon, just south of the city centre, Freemans Park, 90 Aylestone Rd, LE2 7LT, T0871-224 4007, www.odeon.co.uk. Hollywood blockbusters.

Phoenix Arts Centre, 4 Midland St, LE1 1TG, T0116-242 2800, www.phoenix.org.uk. Runs a programme of films, theatre, dance and other performance.

Piccadilly Cinema, 2 Green Lane Rd, Evington, LE5 3TP, T0116-251 8880, www.piccadillycinemas.co.uk. Showing the latest Bollywood releases.

Theatre
Curve Theatre, Rutland St, LE1 1SB, T0116-242 3560, www.curveonline.co.uk. Musicals, plays and pantos.

Festivals

Leicester *p118, map p120*
Feb Dave's Leicester Comedy Festival, www.comedy-festival.co.uk. Held over 2 weeks in the middle of Feb, featuring established stars alongside brand new talent.

May Early Music Festival, www.earlymusicleicester.co.uk. Early Music events held in museums, churches, the cathedral and Castle Park.

Jun Leicester International Music Festival, www.leicesterinternationalmusicfestival.org.uk. Specializes in chamber music.

Aug Leicester Caribbean Carnival, www.leicestercarnival.com. The city's big carnival at the beginning of Aug is a celebration of the Caribbean community in the city.

Nov Leicester stages the biggest **Diwali** celebrations outside India. Marking the start of the Hindu New Year, this festival of light is held at the beginning of Nov, when the 'Golden Mile' is illuminated in spectacular style, the road is closed to traffic and a stage put up at the flyover end for music and dancing, with a firework display as a grand finale.

⊙ Shopping

Leicester *p118, map p120*
Daminis, 87 Belgrave Rd, LE4 6AS,
T0116-266 4357, www.daminis.com.
A cut above the other sari shops for
chic East–West fashions.
The Sangam Pan House, just off the south
end of the strip, 3A Roberts Rd, LE4 5HG,
T0116-266 3436. One of the more luxurious
shops specializing in the mysterious Indian
art of pan, the traditional areca nut pick-me-
up wrapped in a green betel leaf.
Sona, 112-114 Belgrave Rd, LE4 5AT,
T0116-266 1142. www.sonajewellers.com.
For gold jewellery from the subcontinent.
TF Cash & Carry, 93 Belgrave Rd, LE4 6AS,
T0116-266 0946. An underground Aladdin's
Cave, stocking everything from Hindi DVDs
and Indian cooking pots, to life-sized framed
photographs of the Indian master Sai Baba.

⊙ What to do

Leicester *p118, map p120*
Leicester City Football Club, King
Power Stadium, Filbert Way, LE2 7FL,
T0844-815 5000, www.lcfc.com.
Leicester County Cricket Club,
Grace Rd, LE2 8AD, T0871-282 1879,
www.leicestershireccc.co.uk.
The Leicester Tigers, Aylestone Rd, LE2 7TR,
T0844-856 1880, www.leicestertigers.com.
One of the top rugby union sides in the
country, they play at Welford Road.

⊖ Transport

Leicester *p118, map p120*
Bus
National Express, www.nationalexpress.
com, run regularly direct to **Nottingham
Broad Marsh** (5 mins) and direct every
hour or so to **London Victoria**. They also
run direct services 7 times per day to
Birmingham Digbeth (1 hr to 1 hr 30 mins)
and 9 times per day to **Derby** (1 hr).

Car
Avis, 1 Samuel St, LE1 1RU, T0844-544 6071,
www.avis.co.uk. **Thrifty**, 1 Byron St, LE1 3QD,
T0116-262 0444, www.thrifty.co.uk.

Taxi
A1 Airport Taxis, 244 Braunstone La,
LE3 3AS, T0116-289 5353, www.a1airport
cars-leicester.co.uk; **Swift Fox Cabs**, 77a
Church Gate, LE1 3AN, T0116-262 8222,
www.swiftfoxcabs.co.uk.

Train
East Midlands Trains, www.eastmidlands
trains.co.uk, run the regular direct services
to **Nottingham** (35 mins), **Derby**
(30 mins) and **London St Pancras** (1 hr
25 mins). **Cross Country Trains**, www.
crosscountrytrains.co.uk, run the regular
direct service to **Birmingham** (50 mins).

⊙ Directory

Leicester *p118, map p120*
Hospitals Leicester Royal Infirmary,
Infirmary Sq, LE1 5WW, T0300-303 1573

Contents

Footnotes

Index

Titles available in the Footprint *Focus* range

Latin America	UK RRP	US RRP
Bahia & Salvador	£7.99	$11.95
Brazilian Amazon	£7.99	$11.95
Brazilian Pantanal	£6.99	$9.95
Buenos Aires & Pampas	£7.99	$11.95
Cartagena & Caribbean Coast	£7.99	$11.95
Costa Rica	£8.99	$12.95
Cuzco, La Paz & Lake Titicaca	£8.99	$12.95
El Salvador	£5.99	$8.95
Guadalajara & Pacific Coast	£6.99	$9.95
Guatemala	£8.99	$12.95
Guyana, Guyane & Suriname	£5.99	$8.95
Havana	£6.99	$9.95
Honduras	£7.99	$11.95
Nicaragua	£7.99	$11.95
Northeast Argentina & Uruguay	£8.99	$12.95
Paraguay	£5.99	$8.95
Quito & Galápagos Islands	£7.99	$11.95
Recife & Northeast Brazil	£7.99	$11.95
Rio de Janeiro	£8.99	$12.95
São Paulo	£5.99	$8.95
Uruguay	£6.99	$9.95
Venezuela	£8.99	$12.95
Yucatán Peninsula	£6.99	$9.95

Asia	UK RRP	US RRP
Angkor Wat	£5.99	$8.95
Bali & Lombok	£8.99	$12.95
Chennai & Tamil Nadu	£8.99	$12.95
Chiang Mai & Northern Thailand	£7.99	$11.95
Goa	£6.99	$9.95
Gulf of Thailand	£8.99	$12.95
Hanoi & Northern Vietnam	£8.99	$12.95
Ho Chi Minh City & Mekong Delta	£7.99	$11.95
Java	£7.99	$11.95
Kerala	£7.99	$11.95
Kolkata & West Bengal	£5.99	$8.95
Mumbai & Gujarat	£8.99	$12.95

Africa & Middle East	UK RRP	US RRP
Beirut	£6.99	$9.95
Cairo & Nile Delta	£8.99	$12.95
Damascus	£5.99	$8.95
Durban & KwaZulu Natal	£8.99	$12.95
Fès & Northern Morocco	£8.99	$12.95
Jerusalem	£8.99	$12.95
Johannesburg & Kruger National Park	£7.99	$11.95
Kenya's Beaches	£8.99	$12.95
Kilimanjaro & Northern Tanzania	£8.99	$12.95
Luxor to Aswan	£8.99	$12.95
Nairobi & Rift Valley	£7.99	$11.95
Red Sea & Sinai	£7.99	$11.95
Zanzibar & Pemba	£7.99	$11.95

Europe	UK RRP	US RRP
Bilbao & Basque Region	£6.99	$9.95
Brittany West Coast	£7.99	$11.95
Cádiz & Costa de la Luz	£6.99	$9.95
Granada & Sierra Nevada	£6.99	$9.95
Languedoc: Carcassonne to Montpellier	£7.99	$11.95
Málaga	£5.99	$8.95
Marseille & Western Provence	£7.99	$11.95
Orkney & Shetland Islands	£5.99	$8.95
Santander & Picos de Europa	£7.99	$11.95
Sardinia: Alghero & the North	£7.99	$11.95
Sardinia: Cagliari & the South	£7.99	$11.95
Seville	£5.99	$8.95
Sicily: Palermo & the Northwest	£7.99	$11.95
Sicily: Catania & the Southeast	£7.99	$11.95
Siena & Southern Tuscany	£7.99	$11.95
Sorrento, Capri & Amalfi Coast	£6.99	$9.95
Skye & Outer Hebrides	£6.99	$9.95
Verona & Lake Garda	£7.99	$11.95

North America	UK RRP	US RRP
Vancouver & Rockies	£8.99	$12.95

Australasia	UK RRP	US RRP
Brisbane & Queensland	£8.99	$12.95
Perth	£7.99	$11.95

For the latest books, e-books and a wealth of travel information, visit us at:
www.footprinttravelguides.com.

 footprint travelguides.com

 Join us on facebook for the latest travel news, product releases, offers and amazing competitions:
www.facebook.com/footprintbooks.